THE TRUTH ABOUT DEATH AND DYING

THE TRUTH ABOUT DEATH AND DYING

MARK J. KITTLESON, PH.D.
Southern Illinois University
General Editor

WILLIAM KANE, PH.D.
University of New Mexico
Adviser

RICHELLE RENNEGARBE, PH.D.
McKendree College
Adviser

Karen Meyers
Principal Author

☑®
Facts On File, Inc.

The Truth About Death and Dying

Copyright © 2005 by BOOK BUILDERS LLC

Facts On File, Inc.
132 West 31st Street
New York NY 10001

Library of Congress Cataloging-in-Publication Data

Meyers, Karen, 1948–
    The truth about death and dying / Mark Kittleson, general editor; William Kane, adviser; Richelle Rennegarbe, adviser; Karen Meyers, principal author.
        p. cm.
    Includes index.
    ISBN 0-8160-5303-0 (hc : alk. paper)
    1. Death–Social aspects. 2. Death–Psychological aspects. 3. Bereavement. 4. Teenagers and death. I. Kittleson, Mark J., 1952– II. Kane, William, 1947– III. Rennegarbe, Richelle. IV. Title.
    HQ1073.M49 2006
    306.9'03–dc22   2005005796

Facts On File books are available at special discounts when purchased in bulk quantities for businesses, associations, institutions, or sales promotions. Please call our Special Sales Department in New York at (212) 967-8800 or (800) 322-8755.

You can find Facts On File on the World Wide Web at http://www.factsonfile.com

Text design by David Strelecky
Cover design by Cathy Rincon
Graphs by Jeremy Eagle

Printed in the United States of America

MP Hermitage 10 9 8 7 6 5 4 3 2 1

This book is printed on acid-free paper.

CONTENTS

LIST OF ILLUSTRATIONS AND TABLES

PREFACE

In developing The Truth About series, we have taken time to review some of the most pressing problems facing our youths today. Issues such as alcohol and drug abuse, depression, family problems, sexual activity, and eating disorders are at the top of a list of growing concerns. It is the intent of these books to provide vital facts while also dispelling myths about these terribly important and all-too-common situations. These are authoritative resources that kids can turn to in order to get an accurate answer to a specific question or to research the history of a problem, giving them access to the most current related data available. It is also a reference for parents, teachers, counselors, and others who work with youths and require detailed information.

Let's take a brief look at the issues associated with each of those topics. Alcohol and drug use and abuse continue to be a national concern. Today's young people often use drugs to avoid life's extraordinary pressures. In doing so they are losing their ability to learn how to cope effectively. Without the internal resources to cope with pressure, adolescents turn increasingly back to addictive behaviors. As a result, the problems and solutions are interrelated. Also, the speed with which the family structure is changing often leaves kids with no outlet for stress and no access to support mechanisms.

In addition, a world of youths faces the toughest years of their lives, dealing with the strong physiological urges that accompany sexual desire. Only when young people are presented the facts honestly, without indoctrination, are they likely to connect risk taking with certain behaviors. This reference set relies on knowledge as the most important tool in research and education.

Finally, one of the most puzzling issues of our times is that of eating disorders. Paradoxically, while our youths are obsessed with thinness and beauty and go to extremes to try to meet perceived societal expectations, they are also increasingly plagued by obesity. Here, too, separating the facts from fiction is an important tool in research and learning.

As much as possible, The Truth About presents the facts through honest discussions and reports of the most up-to-date research. Knowing the facts associated with health-related questions and problems will help young people make informed decisions in school and throughout life.

Mark J. Kittleson, Ph.D.
General Editor

HOW TO
USE THIS BOOK

NOTE TO STUDENTS

Knowledge is power. By possessing knowledge you have the ability to make decisions, ask follow-up questions, or know where to go to obtain more information. In the world of health, that is power! That is the purpose of this book—to provide you the power you need to obtain unbiased, accurate information and *The Truth About Death and Dying.*

Topics in each volume of The Truth About series are arranged in alphabetical order, from A to Z. Each of these entries defines its topic and explains in detail the particular issue. At the end of most entries are cross–references to related topics. A list of all topics by letter can be found in the table of contents or at the back of the book in the index.

How have these books been compiled? First, the publisher worked with me to identify some of the country's leading authorities on key issues in health education. These individuals were asked to identify some of the major concerns that young people have about such topics. The writers read the literature, spoke with health experts, and incorporated their own life and professional experiences to pull together the most up-to-date information on health issues, particularly those of interest to adolescents and of concern in Healthy People 2010.

Throughout the alphabetical entries, the reader will find sidebars that separate Fact from Fiction. There are Question-and-Answer boxes that attempt to address the most common questions that youths ask about sensitive topics. In addition, readers will find special features called "Teens Speak"–case studies of teens with personal stories related to the topic in hand.

This may be one of the most important books you will ever read. Please share it with your friends, families, teachers, and classmates. Remember, you possess the power to control your future. One way to affect your course is through the acquisition of knowledge. Good luck and keep healthy.

NOTE TO LIBRARIANS

This book, along with the rest of The Truth About series, serves as a wonderful resource for young researchers. It contains a variety of facts, case studies, and further readings that the reader can use to help answer questions, formulate new questions, or determine where to go to find more information. Even though the topics may be considered delicate by some, don't be afraid to ask patrons if they have questions. Feel free to direct them to the appropriate sources, but do not press them if you encounter reluctance. The best we can do as educators is to let young people know that we are there when they need us.

Mark J. Kittleson, Ph.D.

General Editor

LIFE AND DEATH

Psychiatrist Elisabeth Kübler-Ross (1926-2004), author of the best-selling book *On Death and Dying* (1969), has written, "For those who seek to understand it, death is a highly creative force. The highest spiritual values of life can originate from the thought and study of death." What Kübler-Ross means is that human life is made all the more precious and valuable by the fact that it ends. People who avoid the idea of death and pretend that they will never die may not be living life to the fullest. They may postpone crucial spiritual tasks, fritter away time, engage in superficial pursuits, and ultimately fail to fully experience that very brief light called life. Perhaps one of the most compelling literary portrayals of the end of life, "The Death of Ivan Ilych" by the nineteenth-century writer Leo Tolstoy, offers an intimate portrait of a man who has led a superficial life as he realizes that he has no time left:

> It occurred to him that what had appeared perfectly impossible before, namely that he had not spent his life as he should have done, might after all be true. It occurred to him that his scarcely perceptible attempts to struggle against what was considered good by the most highly placed people, those scarcely noticeable impulses which he had immediately suppressed, might have been the real thing, and all the rest false. And his professional duties and the whole arrangement of his life and of his family, and all his social and official interests, might all have been false. He tried to defend all those things to himself and suddenly felt the weakness of what he was defending. There was nothing to defend.

Ivan Ilych never thought about the possibility that he might die and was taken by surprise, unaware of his own mortality. Only at the moment of his death does he realize that he has wasted his life. Ilych is not alone; many people avoid thinking about death, to their own detriment. Adolescents may be particularly susceptible to denying the possibility of death. Because the average age of death in the United States today, according to the National Center for Health Statistics, is 77.2 years, a 16-year-old may feel that old age and the prospect of death are infinitely far away. Young, healthy, and full of vitality, many teens feel they are immortal. Others die, certainly, but—they think—I cannot. This "denial of death" may lead to risk-taking behavior among adolescents. Indeed, the top three causes of death among teenagers are traumatic injuries, particularly car accidents, suicide, and homicide (intentional).

Some adults wish they could preserve the innocence of children forever, never having to introduce the idea of death at all, but as young people become more and more independent, it is important that they understand that death may lurk just around the corner. When adults say to their adolescent children, "These are the best times of your life," they are really saying, "Don't waste a minute of it—it's over too soon." Some parents may wish to protect young people from the idea of death for as long as possible, but youth may be the best time to learn that life is, indeed, short, and that risk-taking is unhealthy, as risks might cause it to be even shorter.

DEATH AND DYING ISSUES

Not more than 100 years ago, it would have been impossible to protect a young person from an intimate knowledge of death. People died young and at home, with family members, including children, at their sides. Mothers and daughters washed the body and prepared it for burial, sometimes laying the body out on the dining room table for viewing. Fathers and sons built a coffin, dug the grave, and buried the body on the family property.

Over the years, advances in medical technology brought about a change in how Americans dealt with death. More and more elderly and sick people died in hospitals, helpless at the end of life, hooked up to machines that breathed for them. Undertakers, also called funeral directors, picked up the body from the hospital so that the next time the family saw their relative, he or she was wearing makeup and dressed and laid out on a mattress in a coffin. Death became something that could be avoided at all costs—which was fine for the living but hard on those who had to die, often alone, in hospital rooms surrounded by strangers.

In 1969, Kübler-Ross revolutionized America's thinking about death when she exposed the awful loneliness and indignity of most hospital deaths. The **hospice** movement, which was begun in England in 1967 by Dame Cicely Saunders, came to the United States in 1974 as a result of the popularity of Kübler-Ross's works. Hospice is based on the idea that when a patient is terminal, continuing to strive for a cure is useless, painful, and undignified. It is, perhaps, better to admit that life is ending and try to find a way to allow the patient to die with dignity. Hospice care allows people to die at home, with sufficient pain medication so that the patient is not suffering but not so much medication that the person is not alert enough to say good-bye to family.

Still, most people today die in hospitals, and many are kept alive by artificial means. As a result, advances in technology have led to a number of ethical dilemmas that have no easy solutions.

RIGHT TO DIE

Before the modern era, when a person's heart and lungs stopped functioning, they were, quite simply, dead. Today, machines can restore heart function and keep lungs working, almost indefinitely, leading to questions about delaying death or extending life for patients with no chance of recovery. In 1975, the story of Karen Ann Quinlan brought to national attention the question of what precisely it meant to be "alive." The young woman was in a "persistent vegetative state" as a result of an overdose of tranquilizers and alcohol. Her parents sought to disconnect her from life support because they hoped she would be spared the indignity of living without higher brain function, connected to machines. Eventually the courts allowed her parents to disconnect their daughter from life support, but she lived another 10 years before dying.

Many other such cases have come to public attention over the years. Jack Kevorkian, a Michigan pathologist who came to be known as "Dr. Death," participated in a number of highly publicized "physician-assisted suicides" in the 1990s. He believed that people who were terminally ill had the right to have a physician help them to die if they chose to do so. Without the help of a physician, said Kevorkian, those who chose suicide might botch the job by not taking enough of a drug or might use methods that create unnecessary pain. Eventually Kevorkian was sentenced to prison in Michigan for second-degree murder and injecting a patient with an illegal drug.

In 1997, Oregon became the first and only state in the United States to legalize **physician-assisted suicide (PAS)**. (PAS is also legal in the Netherlands). In Oregon, a person who is terminally ill may ask a doctor for a prescription that will provide enough of a drug to allow the person to kill himself or herself. The physician is not allowed to administer the drug, only to prescribe it. To date, 171 people in Oregon have opted to die in this manner. However, many people believe that the best result of the law is that doctors now refer more patients to hospice care and know more about **palliative care**, how to help people who are dying avoid pain. Many people fear that such laws will inevitably lead to a "slippery slope" in which society begins to kill people who are too much trouble to deal with—the disabled, poor people who are a financial burden, and so on. In 2003, U.S. Attorney General John Ashcroft sued to overturn the Oregon law. The case is pending and has the support of many religious people and those who are supporters of the **right-to-life** movement—opponents of abortion.

Recently a debate raged between the parents and husband of a woman who had been kept alive by a feeding tube. In 1990, Terri Schiavo suffered a heart attack that led to severe brain damage and was later diagnosed as being in a "persistent vegetative state." Her husband, Michael Schiavo, sued to be allowed to remove the feeding tube from his wife. Terri's parents, Bob and Mary Schindler, believed that Terri was aware of what was going on around her and did not want the feeding tube removed. Many Americans lined up on both sides of the debate. Some people felt that only God could decide when a person dies. People who accepted the doctors' diagnoses held that Terri was being kept alive in a manner inconsistent with human dignity. The courts sided with Michael Schiavo, and shortly after the tubes were removed, Terri died.

EXPENSIVE FUNERALS

Today, the funeral industry is a multibillion-dollar business. Proponents feel it provides an essential service. Funeral directors see themselves as "grief counselors" who create a "memory picture" for grieving families, allowing relatives to get past the death and go on with life. Some critics of the industry believe that funeral directors use underhanded tactics to exploit grief, convincing people to spend extravagantly on funerals when they cannot afford it. A movement exists in the United States today to do away with funeral homes and funeral directors altogether and to go back to earlier, simpler funeral practices, including home burials.

LIVING LONGER

Issues of death and dying will continue to be of concern to Americans as the population ages. In 1900, there were only 3 million Americans over the age of 65; by the year 2030, there will be 70 million. If those older individuals are healthy and productive, the country will benefit. If they live longer but are afflicted with chronic illnesses, the nation's health-care costs will increase greatly. Thus, encouraging people to make lifestyle choices today that will ensure better health tomorrow is a major public-health issue in the United States. More and more research is being conducted in order to help determine what practices contribute to a healthy and productive old age, and researchers are emphasizing that it is never too late to make healthy choices.

RISKY BUSINESS SELF-TEST: TRUE OF FALSE

It is also never too early, of course, to make healthy choices. Young people can begin today to do those things that will not only prolong their lives but also ensure that their "golden years" are truly golden. Even if "old age" is 60 years away, the choices teenagers make now will determine how healthy and productive those years will be.

On a separate piece of paper, record your answers to the following true/false questions. In the blank space beside each statement, give yourself one point for each "true" answer and zero points for each "false" answer.

Physical health (the quality or condition of the body):

_____ I maintain a desirable weight.

_____ I exercise for 30 minutes at least three to four times a week.

_____ I get at least seven to eight hours of sleep each night.

_____ I drink at least five glasses of water daily.

_____ I do not abuse drugs or alcohol.

_____ I consistently wear a seat belt.

_____ I avoid all tobacco products.

_____ I eat a balanced diet with plenty of fruits and vegetables and whole-grain products.

Mental and emotional health (thinking and feeling abilities):

_____ I think about and weigh consequences before I act. (For example, I do not get into a car with someone who has been drinking.)

_____ I learn from my mistakes and do not make the same errors over and over.

_____ I manage my time well so that I am not constantly stressed.

_____ I do not engage in negative self-talk (that is, I do not constantly tear myself down).

_____ I routinely use various stress-reduction techniques.

_____ I am able to express my feelings.

_____ When I am angry, I try to let others know in nonconfrontational ways.

_____ I do not worry constantly.

_____ When I am anxious, I take steps to relax.

_____ I believe others like me for who I am.

_____ I like who I am.

Social health (quality of interactions with others):

_____ I get along well with most people.

_____ Most people like me.

_____ I am a good listener.

_____ I have someone I can talk to about my feelings and problems.

_____ I have a few close friends.

Spiritual health (living a purposeful, meaningful life):

_____ I am content with who I am.

_____ I nurture myself.

_____ I believe that there is meaning to life.

_____ I help others without expecting something in return.

_____ I live each day fully.

Now, total your scores in each category and compare your score to the maximum:

	Maximum Score	Your Score
Physical Health	8	_____
Mental and Emotional Health	11	_____
Social Health	5	_____
Spiritual Health	5	_____
Total	29	_____

A score of 23 to 29 is excellent, especially if your points were equally distributed across all the dimensions of health. A total score of 23 to 29 reveals that your lifestyle is generally healthy across the board. A score of less than 23 may indicate that you are neglecting an essential element of heath. If you feel you need help, or just want to talk to a professional, there are sources available to you in every category. To begin searching for those right for you, see "Hotlines and Help Sites" at the end of this book. Also, consult such entries as Help and Support and Living Longer, Living Better.

A TO Z ENTRIES

■ ABUSE OF THE SICK AND INFIRM

Improper treatment of people who are physically or psychologically impaired is abuse. Those who are supposed to care for people with mental or physical disabilities, or who are chronically ill, sometimes mistreat them. Abuse can lead to death and include any of the following:

- Physical abuse: physical pain or injury resulting from slapping, punching, pushing, kicking, and so forth. Sexual abuse is also considered a form of physical abuse.

- Psychological abuse: verbal or nonverbal behaviors that cause mental or emotional distress. These behaviors include threats, insults, humiliation, manipulation, the withholding of approval, and/or isolation.

- Financial abuse: theft or misuse of another person's money and other assets

- Active neglect: intentionally failing to provide help with basic needs, such as providing food or medication. Being left alone for long periods of time also constitutes active neglect.

- Passive neglect: unintentionally failing to provide basic needs because of the caregiver's ignorance or their inability to perform necessary tasks

ABUSE OF CHILDREN

Among several studies focusing on child abuse, the National Center on Child Abuse and Neglect in a 1992 report, "Child Abuse and Neglect: A Shared Concern," found that children with disabilities are more likely to suffer abuse than other children. One reason may be that children with disabilities may be afraid to report abuse for fear of losing the help they need. Also, children with disabilities are likely to encounter prejudice if they report abuse—many people may consider them less believable than children who do not have disabilities. Some evidence suggests that children with disabilities may not only be more likely to be abused than other children but also to suffer abuse over longer periods of time.

Many children with disabilities are not physically able to defend themselves or communicate what is happening to them. Some may not know the difference between appropriate and inappropriate physical contact. A child who is used to being cared for in almost every aspect of life—including being bathed and taken to the bathroom—may not recognize that a caregiver has crossed the line into sexual abuse.

Sadly, these children are most likely to be abused by parents and other caregivers—the very people whom the children should be able to trust completely. Parents who have little support or who live in poverty may be overwhelmed by the stress of caring for a sick child, and this stress may lead to abuse. Some parents fail to develop a bond with a newborn child who has serious problems, and this lack of a connection may be responsible for instances of mistreatment. In addition, some abuse—particularly cases of neglect—may stem from ignorance, from not knowing what to do for the child or how to do it.

Education is a major factor in preventing the abuse of disabled children—education for caregivers, parents, and the children themselves. Parents and caregivers need to recognize the signs of abuse, and children need to understand when a behavior has crossed the line into abuse. Parents and caregivers also need to become aware that certain forms of neglect are, in fact, a form of abusive.

Providing assistance for overwhelmed caregivers may also be a factor in preventing abuse. Researchers who study this problem are careful never to say anything that would seem to blame the children for the abuse they suffer, yet they also acknowledge that children with extreme behavioral problems or those who require constant care may prove to be too difficult for some caregivers to handle. Ensuring that caregivers know the signs of "burn out" and have someone who can provide relief may also help to prevent the abuse of children with disabilities.

ABUSE OF WOMEN WITH DISABILITIES

A 1999 study of domestic abuse, "National Study of Women with Physical Disabilities," suggests that women with disabilities are as much at risk of domestic violence as the population as a whole, but the nature of the abuse is sometimes related to their infirmities. That is, their abusers—often their husbands—may withhold such equipment as wheelchairs and braces. They may also refuse to provide help with such tasks as getting out of bed or bathing. Women with disabilities were significantly more likely than the general population to suffer emotional abuse and were more likely to be isolated and reluctant to report abuse.

Women with psychiatric problems were much more likely to suffer physical or sexual abuse than male patients with similar disorders. These women were no more likely to have been abused as children than the general population but were much more likely to have been abused as adults.

ABUSE OF THE ELDERLY

Sickness and feebleness may place many elderly individuals at risk of being abused. Studies published in medical and health journals reveal that about 10 percent of people over 65 years of age have been victims of abuse, and up to 5 million of them are abused every year. Elder abuse occurs in every racial and ethnic group and at every income level. Men and women are equally at risk. Indeed, any older person who is sick or infirm may become a victim of elder abuse.

TEENS SPEAK

My Cousin Emotionally Abused My Aunt Jean

I used to believe that abuse of older people meant only physical attacks. My mind changed when Aunt Jean, Dad's 76-year-old sister, told us how she was abused by her son. When she broke her hip, Aunt Jean realized that she needed help with daily tasks. She asked Jim, her only son, who was recently laid off from his job, if he would help her until she could get around by herself.

Because Jim had lost his job and was not going to be able to pay his rent, he agreed to move in with Aunt Jean. He helped her with housekeeping chores and paying bills. Eventually, he asked Aunt Jean to pre-sign blank checks. One day when Aunt Jean was checking her bank statement, she noticed a very large withdrawal and became suspicious of Jim. She confronted him.

Jim accused Aunt Jean of not being grateful for all he was doing for her. He threatened to pack up and leave her all alone. He withheld her mail. Aunt Jean became depressed. She was convinced that she had no way out, but she finally told my Dad what happened and he invited her to stay with us. Although Jim never hit his mother, he still abused her. I still cannot believe how he treated my Aunt Jean.

As is the case with women and children with disabilities, family members are responsible for most elder abuse. The journal *Nursing Older People* reported on a study of 2,000 elderly living in Boston, Massachusetts. Researchers found that a spouse is responsible for 58 percent of all elder abuse, and an adult child for 24 percent. More than half of those who abuse the elderly suffer from alcoholism, drug abuse, or mental problems.

According to the *Mount Sinai Journal of Medicine* (2003), approximately 84 percent of elders do not report their abuse to anyone, mostly because of a fear of being left alone or feelings of shame. Another reason elders may deny or not report abuse is due to their belief that outsiders should not know about their personal business. Although laws against domestic violence and child abuse have long been on the books, new programs are being developed and new laws enacted to help protect the elderly.

Laws

In 1976, psychiatrist Alex Comfort, whose early career was devoted to the study of aging, wrote in *A Good Age*, "Wisdom would suggest that the most foolish . . . prejudice is that directed against a group to which we must all join." In other words, a person who abuses the elderly is perpetrating treatment that may one day happen to him or her.

Today 45 states have laws that require health-care workers to maintain records of reported or suspected elder abuse. In an effort to encourage people to report abuse to authorities, the name of the "whistle-blower" is kept secret. These laws often include consequences for *not* reporting elder abuse. For example, according to the 2003 United States Elder Justice Act, a nursing home operator who fails to report even a "reasonable suspicion" of elder abuse is subject to a fine of up to $200,000. Other laws require that medical workers be trained to recognize elder abuse.

Prevention

In addition to laws, other efforts to prevent elderly abuse include the following strategies:

- Becoming aware that elder abuse exists
- Learning the telltale signs of elder abuse, a few of which include unexplained bruises, burns, or broken bones; difficulty walking; bloody or stained clothing; and depression
- Becoming a leader in the fight to stop abuse of elders, which may include reporting abuse to authorities

See also: Elderly Men, Aging of; Elderly Women, Aging of

FURTHER READING

Brogden, M., and P. Nijhar. *Crime, Abuse, and the Elderly.* UK: Willan Publishers, 2000.

ALTERNATIVE LIVING

Living arrangements for elderly people who can no longer live safely at home is called alternative living. As people get older, many worry about having to move in with their children or live in a nursing home; they fear losing their independence and dignity and dread having to be cared for by others. Yet sooner or later, many elders find themselves physically unable to clean house, drive a car, or handle other daily chores. These elders may need to consider other living arrangements.

As the percentage of Americans over the age of 65 grows, so will the need for alternative living arrangements. Such arrangements might include living with children or other family members or moving into an assisted-living facility or nursing home.

MOVING IN WITH FAMILY

Moving in with family can be less expensive than other alternatives. Even if that were not the case, however, many adult children want to take care of their elderly parents out of a sense of love, duty, or both.

According to a survey conducted by the National Alliance of Care-giving and the American Association of Retired Persons

(AARP) in 1997, people in nearly one in four households are caring for an older relative. Women do most of the day-to-day work of caregiving. Their duties range from running errands to bathing, dressing, and feeding an elderly relative. The demands of that care can be physically, emotionally, and mentally draining. In some cases, caregivers have had to leave their jobs in order to be available to care for a parent full time.

Respite care, short-term or temporary care for an elderly person, can sometimes help to make caregiving easier. It allows the primary caregiver some relief from day-to-day responsibilities.

Although caring for an elderly relative can be difficult at times, such an arrangement suits many people. In some cases adult children reconnect with their parents and the bond between them is strengthened. Having a grandparent in the house can also be beneficial for children, who may learn both respect and compassion for older people.

DID YOU KNOW?

Main Reasons for Family Caregiving

Condition	Percentage of Care Recipients
Aging	15.5
Mobility Problems	10.4
Dementia	9.7
Heart Disease or Condition	9.6
Cancer	8.6
Stroke	7.8
Arthritis	5.8
Diabetes	4.8
Lung Disease	3.4
Blindness or Vision Loss	3.2
Mental or Emotional Illness	2.8
Broken Bones	2.6
Neurological Problems	2.2
High Blood Pressure	2.0

Source: The National Alliance for Caregiving, 1997.

ASSISTED LIVING

Assisted living is a living arrangement in which personal care services such as meals, housekeeping, transportation, and assistance with activities of daily living are available as needed to people who live on their own in a residential facility. Elders in an assisted living complex are still able to live alone, but they may require help with some daily tasks, including meal preparation.

Assisted living arrangements benefit elderly residents in many ways. Among the most important benefits are social activities, such as concerts, Bingo, or card games. Some teens regularly volunteer their time to play games or visit with elders who may themselves become substitute grandparents.

Safety is another benefit of assisted living. Emergency help is readily available with attendants on call 24 hours a day. Thompson Healthcare, an information service provider in the health-care industry, estimates that approximately 30 percent of the people in assisted living facilities are there because of safety concerns. Many elders fear they will be unable to get help if they fall or that they may forget to take necessary medications. These and other safety concerns are lessened when the elderly live in well-managed assisted living facilities.

One day, you might have to help decide about what type of care your elderly parent needs. Such decisions are not easy for anyone to make.

NURSING HOMES

A nursing home is a licensed facility that provides general nursing care to those who are chronically ill or unable to take care of necessary daily living needs. Nursing homes have come a long way in the past hundred years. According to author Linda Zinn, in an article published in *Nursing Home* (December 1999):

> To be old and alone and ill or frail at the beginning of the 20th century was a frightening proposition. While the more fortunate elderly had families to care for them in their homes—or were, perhaps, members of ethnic or religious communities that provided food and shelter to their aged in a private setting—the less fortunate might very well have found themselves in the proverbial poorhouse. And poor it was in every way: poor (if any) sanitation, poor food, poor clothing, poor sleeping arrangements, no nursing care and little, if any, medical care. The impoverished elderly were basically warehoused until they died.

Many people living today still remember visiting relatives in early nursing homes and think of them as places where frail, dying people sit and stare aimlessly. But nursing homes have improved a great deal since those early days. Since 1965, the federal government has set minimum standards for nursing-home care. The Omnibus Budget Reconciliation Act of 1987 included provisions for federal regulation of the quality life for residents of nursing homes. While nursing homes have improved, and some provide excellent care in luxurious settings, according to the National Citizens' Coalition for Nursing Home Reform, as many as one-third of those living in nursing homes today are malnourished or dehydrated due to poorly trained staff and high turnover.

According to a survey conducted by the MetLife Insurance Company in 2000, only about 4–5 percent of elders in the United States are confined to nursing homes at any given time. These seniors are seriously ill and need help with many tasks of daily living. For example, in 2001, the Centers for Disease Control and Prevention (CDC) reported that more than 96 percent of nursing home residents needed help with bathing, about 90 percent with dressing, and almost 60 percent with using the toilet. Almost half have some form of **dementia**, or severe memory loss.

According to a National Nursing Home Survey (1997), most nursing home residents are older than 75, and the average age for people who enter a nursing home is about 82. Because women normally outlive men, there are 75 percent more women in nursing homes than men. The Agency for Healthcare Research and Quality (AHRQ) reports that more than 90 percent of nursing home residents are white.

Armeda Ferrini, a professor of health science, and Rebecca Ferrini, a physician, are the mother-daughter authors of *Health in the Later Years*. They report that slightly more than half of all nursing home residents are recovering from broken hips and most stay less than a year. Only about 4 percent stay more than 10 years.

In selecting a nursing home, relatives of elderly patients must ensure that the facility protects the basic rights of residents. According to the AARP's Nursing Home Bill of Rights, residents should be entitled to:

- Privacy when they sleep, bathe, and dress
- Freedom to go wherever and whenever they want to visit with friends and relatives

- Choice of what they eat or wear
- Control of their money
- The right to chose their own doctor or make decisions about medical treatment

See also: Elderly Men, Aging of; Elderly Women, Aging of

FURTHER READING

Hodges, H. *Circle of Years: A Caregiver's Journal.* Harrisburg, PA: Morehouse Publishing, 1998.

Van Pelt, E. C., and E. C. Cohen. *The House on Beartown Road: A Memoir of Learning and Forgetting.* New York: Random House, 2003.

ATTITUDES TOWARD DEATH, TEENAGE

How young people ages 12–19 typically think about death, whether the prospect of their own death or the death of a friend or family member, is their attitude toward death. As children and youths develop, their attitudes toward death change. According to psychologist Catherine Deering and professor of nursing Lawrence Scahill in *Psychiatric Nursing: Contemporary Practice* (2005), children as young as three have a basic understanding of death, though they do not believe it is permanent. By the age of seven, however, children do understand that death is permanent. Although adolescents know that those they love may die and will not "come back," they are sometimes less convinced that they, themselves, are mortal.

INVINCIBILITY FABLE

The Centers for Disease Control and Prevention (CDC) reports that the three most frequent causes of death among adolescents are injury, (including injuries from car crashes), homicide, and suicide. Psychologists have long known that teenagers have a tendency to take risks and engage in risky behavior, which is why so many die from injury.

In 1967, in an attempt to explain this risk-taking behavior, psychologist Daniel Elkind advanced his theory of adolescent **egocentrism.** Egocentrism refers to the tendency to overfocus on oneself and one's needs. This egocentrism can be seen in many aspects of adolescent behavior. For example, some teenagers become very critical of

DID YOU KNOW?

Leading Causes of Death in the United States by Age

Rank (All Ages)	1-4	5-14	15-24	25-44	45-65	65+
1. Heart disease	Unintentional injuries	Unintentional injuries	Unintentional injuries	Unintentional injuries	Cancer	Heart disease
2. Cancer	Birth defects	Cancer	Homicide	Cancer	Heart disease	Cancer
3. Stroke	Homicide	Homicide	Suicide	Heart disease	Accidents	Stroke
4. Lung disease	Cancer	Birth defects	Cancer	Suicide	Stroke	Lung disease

Source: Centers for Disease Control and Prevention, 2000.

how their parents dress without thinking twice about making insulting remarks, oblivious to the fact that their comments may be hurtful; their egocentrism makes them focus only on their own feelings and ignore those of their parents.

Elkind theorized that, as adolescents develop their cognitive, or mental, abilities, they begin to believe that they are unique—that no one else has the same feelings or experiences. As part of this egocentrism, many adolescents believe in ideas that Elkind has called the "imaginary audience" and the "invincibility fable." A teenager who believes in an imaginary audience thinks that everyone is watching and judging everything he or she does. This concept may help to explain adolescent suicide, in that young people who commit suicide sometimes think they are punishing people who have hurt them. They focus on the reaction of this imaginary audience ("This will show them!") and do not really think through all the consequences of their actions. They understand that death is permanent but almost seem to believe they will still be around to enjoy their revenge.

The invincibility fable is a belief, held by many adolescents, that life's risks do not really apply to them. Thus, a teenage boy may "know" that drinking and driving do not mix, but he may not think the rule applies to him, because he can "hold his liquor." A teenage girl may know that others have contracted HIV or become pregnant as a result of sexual intercourse, but she may believe such consequences cannot happen to her. Thus many teenagers die precisely because they do not believe they can die.

Over the years since Elkind advanced his theory, many studies have been undertaken to further explore its validity. Elkind himself continued to publish and refine his theory through the 1970s and 1980s. Although the theory is still generally accepted, there has been much debate about why adolescents tend to hold these views about the imaginary audience and the notion of invincibility. Those who agree with Elkind (today referred to as the "Old Look" camp) believe that egocentrism occurs as a result of cognitive development. According to Swiss child psychologist Jean Piaget, adolescents enter a phase of cognitive development he calls "formal operations," by which he means they become more and more capable of abstract thought. It is this change in how young people think that Elkind believes leads to egocentrism. "New Look" theorists believe that egocentrism is not the result of changes in how children think but a part of the process by which adolescents begin to define themselves as individuals, separate from their parents. These researchers hope that by understanding the cause of adolescent egocentrism, they can help parents, teachers, and mental-health professionals better channel risk-taking behavior.

One result of understanding adolescent egocentrism, for example, has been a change in public service announcements against cigarette smoking. According to marketing professor Cornelia Pechmann, in her article "What to Convey in Antismoking Advertisements for Adolescents," rather than emphasize that smoking is dangerous, ads now focus on the fact that smoking has a negative impact on appearance. The thinking behind this change of emphasis is that while teenagers may not believe they will die from smoking, they may think twice about the prospect of yellow teeth and bad breath, as these consequences directly affect their self-image and may lead peers to disapprove of them.

TEENS SPEAK

What If I'd Been in That Car?

I can't believe it; Kaitlin is dead. Last night we were all at a party at Jenni's house—and I have to admit we were drinking. Kaitlin didn't seem that wasted, so I wasn't worried about having her drive me home. But after she dropped me off, she lost control of the car on Old Mill Road and smashed into a tree. They said her blood-alcohol level was one and a half times the legal limit. But I swear she didn't seem that drunk. We've been friends since kindergarten and we were going to go to State together. Now she won't go to college, won't become a marine biologist, won't get married, won't have kids. None of the things we dreamed about will happen for her. And I'm scared. When I think I could have still been in that car . . . .

DEATH OF LOVED ONES

While adolescents may not accept the possibility of their own deaths, they certainly understand the finality of death when it takes a parent or friend. According to an article by Columbia University sociologists Grace Christ, Karolynn Siegel, and Adolph Christ published in the *Journal of the American Medical Association* in 2002, nearly 2 percent of children under the age of 18 have experienced the death of a parent. The authors note that adolescents may experience more intense grief than younger children or adults and that they may experience grief in spurts. Adolescents who lose a parent may be particularly devastated by the remaining parent's grief. Young people may find their friends avoid them because these friends are unsure what to say or do. When adolescents return to school and other activities, they may experience guilt when they forget the parent momentarily or enjoy themselves. Adolescents who are experiencing death for the first time may need someone to talk to them about the five stages of grief—denial, anger, bargaining, depression, and acceptance—so that they understand that their emotions are normal and that grief does eventually heal. According to Christ et al., most adolescents find their way through the grieving process within six to 12 months. However, the sociologists note, 17 percent of bereaved adolescents may need professional help in order to return to normal functioning.

Many adolescents are devastated by the loss of a peer because the death of someone so young reminds them of their own mortality. Losing a friend and their own adolescent innocence about death at the same moment may lead to a particularly intense sorrow and depression. Losing a friend to suicide may even lead the teen to thoughts of personal suicide.

URBAN TEENAGERS AND DEATH

Much of what has been said thus far about teenagers' attitudes toward their own mortality and the deaths of loved ones does not apply to inner-city youths who have witnessed a great deal of violence. According to a 1995 study by sociologist Arlene Stiffman, who surveyed 797 young people in St. Louis, Missouri:

- 75 percent of the young people had heard or seen a shooting;
- 50 percent had seen a killing or serious beating;
- 50 percent reported that murders occur in their neighborhood;
- 39 percent had had a friend beaten or killed; and

- 25 percent reported that teachers at their school had been injured by students.

Stiffman also found that 50 percent of the youths surveyed had been in a "serious physical fight" and that 33 percent "had used a weapon in a fight." This exposure to violence has two major consequences for inner-city youths. According to Stiffman, "They see no hope for the future, feel suicidal, and do not know how to escape from the violence except by being violent themselves or numbing themselves with drugs or alcohol." Rather than feeling invincible, many inner–city teenagers believe that they will not live to adulthood. This belief–like the invincibility fable–may lead to risky behavior.

A 1998 article, "Dying and Grieving in the Inner City," notes that many inner-city teenagers must deal with loss as a constant companion. Because they have witnessed so much death from AIDS, drugs, and violence, these young people have a greater experience of loss and how to respond to it and grow through it. They seem to feel less denial of the possibility of loss and less separation from death. While such painful lessons may lead some urban young people to heal more quickly when a loss occurs, it can also cause some teenagers to devalue life–with awful consequences. A case study in the 2000 book, *The Scarred Heart: Understanding and Identifying Kids Who Kill* by psychologist Helen Smith, describes a 12-year-old convicted murderer named Xavier whose lifetime of exposure to violence had left him without the ability to empathize. Quite simply put, he did not see people as possessing qualities that made them unique. After being arrested for murder, he felt it was unfair that he should be locked up for killing someone who had no worth. Why should he be held accountable for taking a life that had no significance to him?

RISK-TAKING BEHAVIOR

Because adolescent risk-taking behavior often results in death, it might seem that risk-taking is by definition a bad thing. Not so, says psychiatrist Lynn E. Ponton in her 1998 book *The Romance of Risk: Why Teenagers Do the Things They Do.* Dr. Ponton maintains that risk taking is actually good for teens and can help them become independent individuals. She suggests that parents should help teens understand their risk-taking behavior and then guide them toward healthy risk taking. For example, teens who seek thrills by using drugs or alcohol might be encouraged instead to try physical activity that can evoke the same feeling–such as rock climbing or white-water rafting (under the supervision of a trained expert).

While a person's age might affect his or her understanding of death, by the teenage years, one becomes aware of the final separation involved. Young people may have difficulties in accepting death, but this is normal. They may also need to overcome unrealistic beliefs about their own mortality, but risky behavior–within reason–is a part of growing up.

See also: Death of a Friend; Death of a Parent; Drug and Alcohol Abuse; Grieving, The Process of; Violent Death

FURTHER READING
Baxter, Grant, and Wendy Stuart. *Death and the Adolescent: A Resource Handbook for Bereavement Support Groups in School.* Toronto: University of Toronto Press, 1998.

■ CREMATION

Cremation is the use of intense heat and flame to dispose of a dead body. Modern cremations subject the body to extremely high temperatures until all that remains are bone fragments and ashes. Before the modern era, cremation involved burning the body on a **pyre,** a heaped pile of wood. Other methods of disposing of dead bodies include burial in the earth (also referred to as **inhumation**) or in a vault of some sort.

HISTORY OF CREMATION

People have been cremating bodies as part of a funeral rite for over 5,000 years. Archaeologists, scientists who study ancient cultures by examining their artifacts, have found urns for holding human remains throughout the British Isles, Europe, and Russia. Cremation was an important part of the ritual of death in Greece about 3,000 years ago. Homer, in the *Iliad* (the epic poem written in about 800 B.C.E.), portrays cremation as the primary method of disposing of the dead and provides elaborate descriptions of two cremations, that of Achilles' friend Patroclus and of his enemy, Hector, who was a Trojan. The heroes of the *Iliad* went to lengths to ensure that the bodies of their fallen comrades were rescued from the battlefield and given a proper funeral. In one of the most moving scenes in the poem, Priam, Hector's elderly father, crosses enemy lines to beg Achilles to release his son's body so that it can be given the honor of cremation.

Romans, in imitation of the Greek custom, began cremating human remains in about 600 B.C.E., and ashes of those who had been cremated were stored in urns and then placed in columbaria, underground vaults with niches designed to hold the urns. Sculptures of the head and shoulders of the deceased were often placed alongside the urns. Many Romans belonged to funeral societies called collegia, which provided a kind of funeral insurance; members paid monthly dues so that the collegia would provide them with a proper burial.

In ancient times Jews did not practice cremation, believing that God commanded them to bury their dead in the earth. Christians, following this tradition, also preferred burial to cremation, as did Muslims. Part of the reason these three religions rejected cremation was their belief in the resurrection of the body. Christians also felt strongly about following the model of burial used by Jesus.

Early Romans and others who persecuted Christians went out of their way to burn Christian bodies on the assumption that doing so would prevent their being resurrected. Although Christian theologians rejected the idea that the body had to be intact in order to be resurrected, their disapproval of cremation may have been, at least in part, a reaction to this practice. As Christianity spread, early church leaders spoke out against cremation as a way of differentiating themselves from pagans. In fact, the shift from cremation to burial as the primary mode of disposing of human remains was seen as a sign that the process of conversion to Christianity was complete. Some exceptions to the ban on cremation were made, however. During times of plague, when thousands of people died within days of one another, bodies were burned. Burying so many in a short period of time would have been impossible, and corpses could not be left to rot.

While Christians eliminated the practice of cremation in much of Europe, many Eastern religions continued to burn remains. Most associated fire with the idea of purification, believing that the remains of the deceased were purified by fire and readied for the afterlife. Modern Hindus, Buddhists, Sikhs, and Jains practice cremation much as their ancestors did. Buddha was cremated, setting an example for many of his followers. Hindus place remains in an urn or set the urn to float upon the sacred river Ganges in India. Japanese Buddhists encourage relatives to pick up a piece of bone with chopsticks and place it in a white jar to take home. Sikhs believe cremation helps to free the soul from the earth.

Modern cremation began in the 1870s, when an Italian professor known only as Brunetti invented a furnace called a retort, which used heat to reduce the body to ash and bone. Unlike ancient funeral pyres, the retort was enclosed so that mourners would not witness the disposal of the body. Sir Henry Thompson, physician to Britain's Queen Victoria, was an advocate for cremation. He felt it was more sanitary than burials. He also regarded cremation as a way to prevent crowding in urban cemeteries. Thompson's article, "Cremation: The Treatment of the Body after Death," published in 1874 in the *Contemporary Review,* generated interest in the practice in both Britain and North America.

Francis Julius LeMoyne, a physician, built the first **crematory,** or facility for cremation, in the United States in Washington, Pennsylvania. The first person cremated there was Baron Joseph Henry Louis Charles DePalm, an Austrian immigrant, on December 6, 1876. By 1913, the United States had 52 crematories. More than 10,000 people were cremated that year.

In 1963, the Roman Catholic Church removed its objections to cremation and allowed Catholics to be cremated if they so wish, as do most Protestant sects and some Reform Jewish congregations. Muslims and most traditional Jews, however, continue to forbid the practice.

TEENS SPEAK

Our Family Plot Is Full, So We're Considering Cremation

Our family has always prided itself in staying together—in death as well as life. For many years all of the people in my family who have died have been buried within our own family section in one of the city's cemeteries.

Recently, my parents said that only one plot remains in the cemetery section belonging to our family and that, if we want to stay together after death, we may have to consider cremation.

Cremation? How could they even consider that? No one in our family has ever been cremated. At every funeral I ever attended, the minister always said something about people coming from the earth and being returned to it.

When I explained my concerns to my mother, she told me that cremation was just one choice. "We could," she said, "possibly purchase another family plot in another close-by cemetery." She also suggested that I search the Internet for information about cremation.

After searching online, I found out some things I did not know about cremation. I found out that people can still donate their organs and that their ashes, called cremains, can be distributed among family members to be made into necklaces or pens. And since you can bury ashes, I guess you are still being returned to the earth. Even though I'm still not sure that cremation is what our family should do, I am willing to find out more.

THE PROCESS OF CREMATION

Cremation usually takes place after a funeral rite, such as a church service, has been completed. In fact, both the Catholic and Jewish faiths recommend that the body—not merely ashes—be present for the funeral service. When the service ends, the body is taken to a crematory and placed in a casket or other container. If a casket is used, all noncombustible material, such as clasps and latches, are removed before being placed in the furnace chamber. Anything on the body that will not burn, such as jewelry, is removed before cremation. According to the law in most places, only one body can be cremated at a time, in order to ensure that the ashes received by the family are, in fact, those of their relative.

The casket is placed in the cremation chamber, where it is consumed by intense heat, with temperatures ranging between 1,400 and 1,800 degrees Fahrenheit. Depending on the size and weight of the remains, the process may take from one to three hours.

Fact Or Fiction?

Vaults are required for the preservation of cremated remains.

Fact: The remains may stay in the box that comes from the crematory, placed in an urn, or scattered. It is legal to scatter ashes on private property in all 50 states, with the property owner's permission.

When cremation is complete and the remains have cooled, the ashes (which are actually bone fragments) are swept from the chamber. All material that has not burned (such as gold fillings or jewelry that was left on the body) is collected and kept by the crematorium. The ashes of the deceased will then be placed in an urn; if bone fragments are too large to fit, they will be ground down to size. Human remains weigh from three to nine pounds after cremation. The urn containing the remains is returned to the family to be placed in a columbarium, buried, or scattered—depending on the wishes of the deceased.

At least two people, former Harvard professor Timothy Leary and Gene Roddenberry, creator of the television series *Star Trek*, have had their remains sent into outer space. Some people place ashes into pendants, which they wear. A British company compresses remains to create a synthetic diamond. According to their advertisements, "A LifeGem is a certified, high quality diamond created from the carbon of your loved one as a memorial to their unique and wonderful life." These synthetic diamonds come in different colors because, the company claims, "the elements and impurities in your loved one's carbon directly affect the resulting color of your LifeGem(s)."

CREMATION STATISTICS

About 10,000 cremations took place in the United States in 1913; in 1975 the number had risen to 150,000. By 2001, the number of cremations had risen to 650,697, which is approximately 27 percent of all deaths that year, according to each state's health department. The Cremation Association of North America publishes cremation statistics by state. Western states have the highest rate of cremation, while southern states have the lowest. In Japan, 97 percent of bodies are cremated. Great Britain, at 70 percent, and the Scandinavian countries, at 65 percent, also have high rates of cremation.

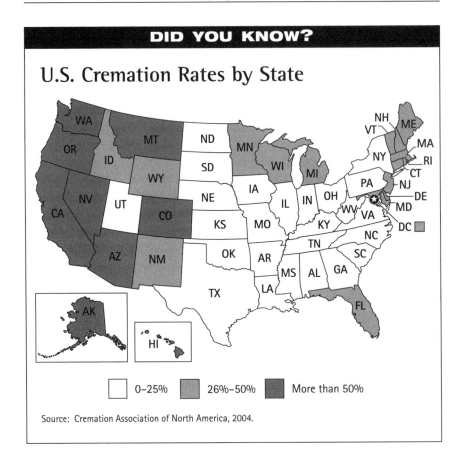

DID YOU KNOW?

U.S. Cremation Rates by State

0–25% 26%–50% More than 50%

Source: Cremation Association of North America, 2004.

See also: Death and Dying, The Business of; Traditions and Death

FURTHER READING
Prothero, Stephen. *Purified by Fire: A History of Cremation in America.* Berkeley: University of California Press, 2002.

■ DEATH, UNEXPECTED AND PLANNED

Grief does not follow a clear path, and everyone grieves differently and for different lengths of time. There are, however, certain factors that appear to influence the intensity and path of grief. For example, the nature of the relationship with the person who has died has an effect on the nature of grief. Surprisingly, if the relationship was good, the grieving process may actually be easier than if there were unresolved issues between the survivor and the deceased.

The age of the person who has died may also have an impact. Grieving is often easier and less complicated when the person who died has lived a long life than when a young child dies. The death of an elderly person seems to be part of the natural course of life, while the death of a child seems unnatural and shocking.

Another important factor that affects the process of grieving is whether or not the death was expected. Many grief therapists and psychologists have suggested that a sudden, unexpected death is much more difficult for survivors to deal with than one that was anticipated.

It is important to note, however, that these are generalizations. An adult who loses an aged parent may be just as devastated as a mother who loses a son in a car accident. And not all researchers agree that an anticipated death is easier to cope with than a planned one. Many factors may intervene.

PLANNED DEATH

According to James Hallenbeck in the 2003 book *Palliative Care Perspectives*, when people know that someone they love is dying, they experience anticipatory grief; that is, they prepare for death in part by mourning the various losses they expect to feel as a result of the death. According to "Loss, Grief, and Bereavement," published in 2003 by the Abramson Cancer Center of the University of Pennsylvania, anticipatory grief has many of the same symptoms as those experienced after a death has occurred. These feelings include all the emotional, cultural, and social reactions that the family and the dying person experienced while expecting death.

Painful as anticipatory grief may be, it may also help with the process of grieving, because the family can begin to get used to the idea of the loss. Family members can complete unfinished business, including sharing memories of the person's life and saying good-bye. Abramson Cancer Center researchers note, however, that anticipatory grief does not always occur when family members know a relative is dying. Similarly, the experience of anticipatory grief does not mean that the period of grieving after the death will be shorter. Additionally, anticipatory grief may cause changes in the feelings of family members toward the person who is dying. In some cases, grieving brings the family closer to the person who is dying. However, there are cases in which a family preparing for the loss may actually draw away from the dying family member, leaving him or her feeling abandoned.

When family members know that someone they love is dying, they have the opportunity to complete many practical arrangements that survivors of an unplanned death cannot. They can discuss the funeral service to ensure that they are following the wishes of the dying person. They can ensure that the will is ready and legal so that unexpected problems do not arise after the death. Thus, the family is not left with loose ends and unspoken feelings.

Not every family will be able to accomplish all of these tasks, however, even if the death is anticipated. Some people refuse to face what is happening, sometimes believing it is morbid to discuss wills and funerals before death. The person who is dying may not want to or be able to deal with these issues.

UNPLANNED DEATH

According to the Abramson Cancer Center article, the grief that follows an unplanned death is quite different from anticipatory grief. An unplanned loss may overwhelm the coping abilities of survivors, making normal functioning impossible. Mourners may not be able to realize the total impact of their loss. Even though people recognize that the loss has occurred, they may not be able to accept the loss mentally and emotionally. Responding to unexpected death, a mourner may feel that the world no longer has order and does not make sense.

Unplanned death may come in a variety of forms, many of them violent. A young man may be killed in a drive-by shooting. A teenage girl may overdose on drugs. A middle-age woman may commit suicide. A child may be hit by a car. How the sudden death occurs has an immense impact on the way those who live on deal with the loss.

Kenneth J. Doka, a professor of gerontology and a bereavement consultant to Hospice Foundation of America, says that "each type of unexpected or violent death poses its own unique problems, intensifying the survivor's grief and heightening his or her sense of vulnerability. Fortunately, most deaths are not sudden and unplanned." The Center for Advanced Palliative Care (CAPC) reports that fewer than 10 percent of people who die each year do so without any warning. The primary causes of such deaths are heart attacks and injuries. According to the National Vital Statistics Report for 2002, injury-related deaths, which account for approximately 4 percent of deaths annually, include such events as automobile accidents, falls, drowning, medical errors, and accidental shootings.

Whatever the cause, when death is unplanned, shock and grief can be intensified because the mourners have not had a chance to say good-bye or make amends for slights and hurts that may have occurred during the lifetime of the deceased. Surviving family members may not know what kind of funeral the deceased wanted; they may have to deal with complicated financial situations without needed information or guidance; and they may have other unfinished business to complete. These factors can delay family members from experiencing grief for a period of time and in fact, may extend and complicate the grieving period.

If, in addition to being unexpected, the death was traumatic and violent in some way—such as an automobile or plane crash—the grieving becomes even more complicated. In a 2000 article, "Sudden Death in Disasters and Transportation Accidents," published in the *Internet Journal of Rescue and Disaster*, social worker John D. Weaver notes that survivors may feel guilt, asking themselves such questions as, "Why did I let him go?" or "What if I had been there?" They may also feel angry at the other driver, the airline, or anyone else who may have been involved with the particular incident. Survivors may also have to deal with media coverage, which can be painful and distracting.

TEENS SPEAK

I Couldn't Handle It When My Dad Died

My dad was a corporate pilot. Last year, the plane he was flying crashed, killing everyone on board. He was only 48, and I was 17. This was the worst thing that ever happened to me. I loved my dad so much, but he and I had been arguing a lot lately and I never got to say I was sorry.

One of the toughest parts of this nightmare was accepting that he was really dead. Dad traveled a lot, so it wasn't unusual for him to be gone from home for days at a time. The whole thing really hit me like a ton of bricks when they towed his car home from the airport—the car was there and he wasn't. That's when I knew he wasn't coming back.

As bad as all this was, something that made dealing with Dad's death even harder was the way the media covered the crash. Dad used to say that when a plane crashes, the first thing the news people do is blame the pilot. And when the investigation is finished and it turns out the pilot was not at fault, "the story will be on the back page where no one will ever see it."

He was right—that was exactly what happened. The day of the crash, we had reporters calling and asking if Dad was drunk, and there were stories in the paper that said he was at fault. I didn't believe any of it, but it hurt so much to have him gone and to have people reading bad things about him.

The National Transportation Safety Board report came out eight months later, and it said the pilot and crew did everything right and the accident was unavoidable. I knew this in my heart all along.

Thoughts of revenge may become overwhelming. Family members can display an unquenchable desire for details of the accident. In his article, Weaver notes that providing the family with all the facts they need is important for them to be able to cope but adds that some individuals obsess over the details, worrying about how much and precisely how the family member suffered.

According to physician and social worker Kristi A. Dyer, in her 2003 article "Dealing with Sudden, Accidental, or Traumatic Death," such losses are even harder to overcome if the grieving family member was also involved in the accident or disaster. These individuals may be haunted by memories of the accident at the same time they are struggling to recover from injuries. Memories of the accident or disaster may dominate the minds of family members. They may be haunted by "survivor's guilt," wondering why they were spared and if they might have done something to prevent the accident. In fact, there are five factors that determine the nature of a sudden loss and that may complicate the grieving process, according to Dr. Dyer. They are:

- Intentionality. To what extent was the death intentional? In other words, was it a homicide, in which someone deliberately took the life of the family member? Or was it a suicide, in which the family member deliberately took his or her own life?

■ Natural or human-caused. When a relative is killed in a natural disaster, survivors may be angry at themselves or at God. If a human caused the death, survivors may focus their anger on the perpetrator.

■ Preventability. If a survivor believes the death could have been prevented, guilt or anger may be overwhelming.

■ Suffering. If the death was painful, survivors may obsess over how much the deceased must have suffered. If the death was quick and painless, some survivors may be grateful that the deceased did not have to undergo pain.

■ Scope. Large-scale disasters such as September 11 and the tsunami that struck Southeast Asia in December of 2004 can affect the intensity of grief. In some cases, according to Dr. Dyer, the outpouring of support and sympathy that may accompany highly publicized disasters may help people through the grieving process. In other situations people may be completely overwhelmed by the scope of the loss.

Unplanned death forces surviving family members to deal with a myriad of emotions other than grief and a considerable number of problems other than the death itself. These factors can lead to what therapists call "complicated grief," sorrow that does not follow the normal patterns and may lead to long-term problems, including health problems and substance abuse.

Some survivors even develop full-blown **post-traumatic stress disorder (PSTD)**. According to the National Center for Post-Traumatic Stress Disorder, PSTD is a psychological condition that can involve nightmares, flashbacks, sleep difficulty, feelings of detachment, substance abuse, depression, confusion, memory loss, and a whole complex of other physical and psychological problems.

COPING WITH UNPLANNED DEATH

Barbara Rubel, director of the Griefwork Center, contributed to the 1999 book *Crisis and Loss*. She notes that in the face of sudden and violent death, immediate grief-crisis intervention can be the key to helping survivors get through the disaster without suffering long-term debilitating problems. Rubel concludes that people who suffer sudden and violent loss might never fully recover from the traumatic event. Feeling grief becomes a part of their being in a lifelong process.

Q & A

Question: Does it help bereaved people recover from the violent death of a family member if they can donate organs from the deceased to help others?

Answer: For some people, organ donation is a way to keep a part of the person who has died alive, and these individuals sometimes even want to get to know the recipients of the organs and their families. So for some families, the answer is "yes," organ donation can help.

Other families, however, may be uncomfortable with the idea and perhaps feel their relative has "suffered enough." Some families are uncomfortable with the idea even if the deceased has filled out an organ donation card.

Crisis intervention can help survivors cope, however. Rubel states that adolescents in particular are in need of intervention after experiencing the violent death of someone they love. If they do not receive the needed help, she notes, young people may experience long-term depression, an inability to separate from parents as they should, problems with making friends and sustaining friendships, and an inability to adjust to college life. The good news is that with adequate help, including individual counseling, support groups, and other kinds of intervention, most people do eventually find a way to cope.

See also: Grieving, The Process of; Help and Support; Violent Death

FURTHER READING
Doka, Kenneth J. *Living with Grief: After Sudden Loss.* Washington, D.C.: Hospice Foundation of America, 1996.

■ DEATH AND DYING, THE BUSINESS OF

The business of death and dying involves the practices for profit of various industries that provide services to the families of those who have died. Funeral homes help bereaved families plan burial services, usually at a time of great vulnerability, when they need comfort, courtesy, and guidance. Funeral home personnel sometimes know the family members personally and have an active involvement in their communities.

However, the industry is also known for unscrupulous business practices. In 1963, Jessica Mitford published *The American Way of Death,* an exposé in which she revealed that many funeral directors took advantage of grieving families to convince them to spend huge amounts of money on the funerals of family members who had died. For example, although **embalming** was not required by law, many funeral directors embalmed bodies routinely, adding to the cost of a funeral. If families knew enough to object and indicate they did not want their relative to be embalmed, some funeral directors would lie, claiming that the practice was required by law.

Fact Or Fiction?

Embalming is necessary to help prevent the spread of disease.

Fact: There is no health purpose served by the practice of embalming. The only people who actually face a health hazard from dealing with a dead body are embalmers themselves, because of their exposure to toxic chemicals. Jesse Carr, chief of pathology at San Francisco General Hospital and professor of pathology at the University of California Medical School, says that a dead body is much less hazardous to health than a live one. According to Carr, a dead person doesn't excrete, inhale, exhale, or perspire. In the past when people died of communicable diseases such as typhoid, cholera, or the plague, illness was spread not from direct contact with the body but through seepage from graves into a city's water supply. In any case, disease-causing organisms cannot be killed by embalming.

Some funeral homes have a history of refusing to show inexpensive caskets in an attempt to convince families to spend more. If a family insisted on seeing the least expensive models, they would often be taken to a dingy back room where they were shown caskets deliberately constructed to look cheap and flimsy. Some funeral directors would try to make family members feel guilty for considering cost "at a time like this." Mitford noted that the average bill for a casket and the various services performed by funeral homes was $750 in 1961.

Just before her own death in 1996, Mitford revised *The American Way of Death,* noting that the average bill for funeral home services in the 1990s had risen to $4,700 before counting the costs of a burial vault, flowers, clothing, clergy and musician fees, and cemetery charges. Adding these expenses to an undertaker's bill brought the total average cost for an adult's funeral to $7,800.

In a 1999 article, Steve Wiegand and Steve Gibson reported in the newspaper *Sacramento Bee* that the average funeral costs nearly $10,000. Here are some itemized costs of a contemporary $10,000 funeral:

- A $1,595 non-declinable fee, to cover everything from a funeral director's advice to the cost of the parking lot
- A Cashmere Beige copper casket with a Champagne Velvet interior ($4,350)
- A standard cemetery plot ($3,300)
- Embalming, dressing, fixing the hair, and "casketing" the deceased ($460)
- Digging the grave ($475)
- Gloves for the pallbearers ($129)
- Underwear for the deceased ($20)

The Federal Trade Commission (FTC) offers a lower estimate for the cost of the average American funeral—$6,000. Even at that lower estimate, however, a funeral is the third-largest expenditure most people will make in their lifetimes, exceeded only by the cost of a home and a car. Not surprisingly, then, the funeral industry is big business, earning an estimated $25 billion a year.

Too many funeral homes?

One reason funeral homes may overcharge customers is the fact that there may be more of these operations than are needed in a locality. With insufficient numbers of customers, funeral directors must

DID YOU KNOW?

National Comparison of Funeral Homes: Needed Versus Existing

State	Needed	Existing	State	Needed	Existing
Alabama	186	404	Montana	33	77
Alaska	13	19	Nebraska	62	232
Arizona	173	146	Nevada	71	43
Arkansas	112	287	New Hampshire	39	91
California	878	771	New Jersey	294	729
Colorado	118	170	New Mexico	59	75
Connecticut	117	297	New York	629	1,850
Delaware	28	66	North Carolina	294	720
DC	22	30	North Dakota	24	100
Florida	674	755	Ohio	439	1,132
Georgia	266	651	Oklahoma	141	379
Hawaii	36	21	Oregon	124	171
Idaho	42	73	Pennsylvania	506	1,801
Illinois	422	1,213	Rhode Island	40	102
Indiana	224	649	South Carolina	152	405
Iowa	113	476	South Dakota	29	107
Kansas	99	326	Tennessee	228	456
Kentucky	160	494	Texas	616	1,201
Louisiana	171	299	Utah	54	85
Maine	50	125	Vermont	20	59
Maryland	179	245	Virginia	233	465
Massachusetts	223	628	Washington	179	199
Michigan	347	731	West Virginia	84	279
Minnesota	150	430	Wisconsin	185	544
Mississippi	116	293	Wyoming	17	32
Missouri	221	595			

Source: Funeral Consumers Alliance, 2004.

extract as much profit as possible from the ones they do have. The Funeral Consumers Alliance, a consumer protection group, compared how many funeral homes states needed, based on the 2004 report from the National Center for Health Statistics and a 2003 report on existing funeral homes in *Funeral Services Insider*, a trade publication for **morticians**. Many states had two and even three times as many funeral homes as were needed.

Funeral conglomerates

In *The American Way of Death Revisited*, Jessica Mitford identifies the growth of huge conglomerates in the funeral industry as one of the major changes in the 30 years since she wrote her first book on the subject. There are several publicly traded companies that dominate the industry: Service Corporation International (SCI), Stewart Enterprises, Loewen Group, Alderwoods Group, and Carriage Services. Most people have never heard of these companies because part of their business strategy is to work behind the scenes to dominate the funeral industry. SCI and the other large "death-care" organizations buy up family-owned funeral homes in a given city, but they do not change the names or, in many cases, the staff. Thus, funeral customers usually do not realize that the local funeral home is no longer a local company, and the conglomerates gain the reputation and customer base of the established funeral home. After having bought a number of independent funeral homes, the conglomerates generally consolidate the business and purchase allied businesses. According to Mitford, a company like SCI buys carefully selected funeral homes, cemeteries, flower shops, and **crematoria** in a particular metropolitan area. The company then clusters the business elements in a central depot, where hearses, limousines, utility cars, drivers, dispatchers, embalmers, and even accounting and data services are combined for a half-dozen formerly independent funeral homes at tremendous savings.

This business operating strategy, which some writers have referred to as "McFuneral," leads to substantially lower costs for the conglomerates. Instead of passing these substantial savings on to consumers, however, the conglomerates actually increase prices. According to Mitford, in places such as Houston, Texas, where SCI cornered 75 percent of the market, prices rose by as much as 60 percent. A study conducted by the New York City Department of Consumer Affairs in 1999 determined that the cost of Jewish funerals in Manhattan had increased by 50 percent after SCI bought five of the six Jewish funeral homes there.

These death-care businesses are so profitable, in fact, that many financial advisers are encouraging people to invest in the industry.

According to a 2001 article in *The San Diego Daily Transcript*, investors have profited from the growth of these death-care companies. While most of the stock market had been in decline at that time, these stocks posted significant gains. Brokerage firms warn that two factors could cause problems for these industries, a lowering in the death rate (which, in fact, occurred in 2002, when the death rate dropped from 855 deaths per 100,000 to 847 per 100,000) and the rise in the number of cremations, which are less profitable. Considerable profit, however, will be made from the rising generation of baby boomers. According to the Goldman Sachs brokerage house, the aging of this generation should enable the death-care industry to experience an extremely stable demand for the future.

PREPAID FUNERALS

The other major change in the death-care business in the past 30 years is the sharp rise in the number of prepaid funeral plans. The **American Association of Retired Persons (AARP)** estimates that Americans spend $25 billion annually on prepaid funerals, up from $18 billion from just 10 years before. Many people prepay for funerals in order to shelter or protect assets so they can be eligible for Medicaid. Faced with ever-rising funeral costs, people also purchase pre-need funeral packages because they believe they can lock in a lower price by prepaying.

While prepaid funerals result in reduced costs in some cases, Mitford notes in *The American Way of Death Revisited* that more and more pre-need plans include an escape clause recommended by a trade journal, *Funeral Insider*. This clause reads, "If the death benefits are less than the current retail price at the time of death, an additional amount of funds will be due." Such a clause obliterates any savings that might have otherwise been realized. Mitford also notes that prepaid funeral plans usually do not cover "cash advance" items, such as an obituary, flowers, and cemetery expenses. Such additional items are then priced in such a way as to make up for any difference between the prepayment and the prevailing cost for a funeral. She cites an example in which an SCI-operated funeral home in Denver charged $200 to send four faxes.

Another problem with prepaying funeral plans is that one has no guarantee that the money will actually be available at the time of death. Most states require that money for prepaid funerals be held in trust to prevent the possibility of fraud, but the laws often have loopholes. Lee Norrgard, consumer affairs analyst for the AARP, in a 1992 report, *Making End-of-Life Decisions*, questions whether adequate consumer protection exists for buyers of pre-need plans. Regulations, investigations, and auditing are minimal in most states. In her book, Mitford notes, "When you make out a check to the mortuary to pay for a pre-need funeral, there is *no* guarantee that the money will find its way to safe-keeping."

Mitford also points out that the industry has a tendency to change casket styles frequently, in some cases as often as every six months. If one preordered the casket Cashmere Beige, for example, and that casket is no longer made at the time of death, the increased cost of the newer version will be added to the bill.

Far preferable to prepaid funeral plans, many financial experts say, is a pay-on-death trust account, sometimes called a **Totten Trust**. This allows money for a funeral to be sheltered for Medicaid eligibility and ensures that the money will be there when it is needed. Mitford and others emphasize that it is always a good idea to preplan a funeral but not to pay for it in advance, unless it is through a trust.

QUESTIONABLE BUSINESS PRACTICES

In the first edition of *The American Way of Death*, Mitford's identification of a number of questionable business practices in the funeral industry led the Federal Trade Commission (FTC) to develop the "Funeral Rule," a series of regulations designed to protect consumers. According to Mitford, during the past 30 years those rules have been watered down, altered, and ignored, resulting in no real improvement in business practices overall. One of the provisions of the Funeral Rule, for example, required that bills must be itemized, so that consumers would know exactly what they were buying. In 1994, however, the FTC amended the rule to allow funeral homes to add a non-declinable fee, to cover a variety of items such as insurance, taxes, staff salaries, maintenance of common areas (including the parking lot), and an unrestricted allowance for profit. This approved fee essentially brought back package pricing for funerals and an upward spiral of prices and profits for funeral directors.

Lisa Carlson, executive director of the Funeral Consumers Alliance (FCA), attended a session of a funeral industry workshop called "How to Add $1,400 to Your Cremation Calls." The speaker promoted a practice called "identification viewing," which involves forcing the family to "identify" the body just prior to cremation—resting in a plain cardboard box. According to the speaker, this practice often provokes the family to say, "Maybe we should get something a little bit nicer," meaning they will spend $2,000 more for a fancier casket. In fact, it is in the sale of caskets that the funeral industry makes its most substantial profits. Bought wholesale from casket companies that refuse to sell to anyone but funeral directors, caskets are marked up from 300 to 500 percent by the funeral homes and cost from $2,000 to $10,000 or more. In recent years, thanks partly to the Internet, many casket companies now sell directly to customers, and funeral homes, by law, are not allowed to refuse to accept them. Other questionable practices include having cemetery plot salespeople roam cemeteries on those days when visitation is highest. There they approach grieving family members to try and sell them plots near a loved one.

Q & A

Question: Why are caskets so expensive?

Answer: Aside from the 300–500-percent markup funeral homes routinely add to the price, some caskets have some rather fancy finishes and equipment. Batesville Casket Company says of its Valley Forge model: "Its charm lies in the warm beauty of the natural grain and finish of finest maple hardwoods." The Monaco is a metal casket "with Sea Mist Polished Finish, interior richly lined in 600 Aqua Supreme velvet, magnificently quilted and shirred, with matching jumbo bolster and coverlet." Another model boasts "quality mattress fabric" making it "soft and buoyant." Batesville says of its bronze caskets that they "combine quality construction and beautiful finishes. Many families choose bronze because it is superior to all other casket materials in strength, durability and naturally non-rusting qualities."

Mitford reports that many funeral directors have a strategy they use routinely to exclude clergy who accompany families to the funeral home from the casket-buying decision. As the family is brought into the showroom, the funeral director pretends to have an issue of importance and asks to speak with the priest, minister, or rabbi in private. Funeral directors, it seems, have learned through bitter experience that members of the clergy tend to dissuade family members from spending large amounts on caskets and counsel them to focus on the spiritual aspects of death.

ALTERNATIVES

In recent years, some people have begun to question the need for a funeral industry in the first place. A hundred years ago, funerals were family affairs. Family members washed the body, built a simple wooden coffin, and dug the grave. The body, if it was laid out for a time, was kept in the house so that family and friends could pay respects. The family drove the body by cart to the graveyard. The costs were no more than the price of wood and nails to make the coffin.

Funerals in England still retain this basic simplicity. In her book, Jessica Mitford points out that the idea of an open coffin for viewing is repugnant to the British; that flowers are typically picked from the family garden, not sent by friends in elaborate arrangements; and that those who attend services and accompany the body to the grave-yard are usually only close members of the family. People do not rou-tinely attend the funerals of coworkers, for example. Americans, however, have become more distant from death over the years. People tend to die in hospitals and nursing homes, the body is prepared by embalmers and cosmetologists, and funeral arrangements are placed in the hands of "professionals."

Recently, however, a number of groups and individuals have begun to advocate a return to the old ways of dealing with the dead. The guide to this movement is Lisa Carlson's 1998 book, *Caring for Your Own Dead: Your Final Act of Love.* Her central idea is that there is no reason to turn the care of the dead over to professionals. Rather, car-ing for the body of a relative is an act of love that itself promotes healing in a way that a packaged funeral cannot. Carlson's book also offers a listing of laws state-by-state so that people can learn which funeral practices are legal in their states and which are not. Many people might be surprised to learn that in most states it is perfectly legal to bury a relative on one's own property and to go through the entire funeral process without the involvement of a funeral director. The only professional required is a doctor to sign the death certificate.

People who agree with Carlson have begun to make coffins for their deceased relatives out of wood or cardboard—which they then decorate with drawings and symbols that remind them of the family member. In an interview on National Public Radio, reporter Jacki Lyden interviewed George Foy, who refused to turn his month-old son over to the funeral industry when he died. Foy described the coffin he built: "I put stuff in the bottom of the box like sand from the beach and beach grass and flowers and a stuffed lamb. And I painted a little picture of a tugboat on the front of it, because when he was alive, he'd always remind me of a tugboat in the fact that he was kind of small but tough and stubborn and cute."

The National Death Care Project, founded in 1996, helps families who want to handle the death of a relative without involving funeral homes and directors. The Funeral Consumers Alliance (FCA) calls itself "a nonprofit organization dedicated to protecting a consumer's right to choose a meaningful, dignified, affordable funeral." The FCA is an extremely useful resource for individuals planning funerals, whether at home or though the use of a funeral home. The FCA lists an incredible wealth of information on its Web site, http://www.funerals.org, and can help families find their way through the tangle of laws in their state.

See also: Death and Money

FURTHER READING
Mitford, Jessica. *The American Way of Death Revisited.* New York: Vintage, 1998.

■ DEATH AND MONEY

Dying in the United States in the 21st century is expensive. Medical and other expenditures to care for dying patients can impose heavy financial burdens on families. Funerals are also quite costly. Estate taxes can create difficulties for some families.

END-OF-LIFE CARE

According to the testimony of Donald Hoover, a professor of statistics at Rutgers University, before the Senate Subcommittee on Appropriations in June 2003, between 1992 and 1996, medical costs during the final year of life averaged $40,000 per person. Medicare, a federal health-insurance program for the disabled and elderly, paid about 70 percent of those costs. The cost of "formal long-term care" (that is, nursing home and hospice care, as opposed to hospitalization) was $137 billion in 2000, 45 percent of which was covered by Medicare. In all, about 25 percent of all Medicare expenditures nationwide are for elderly people in the final year of their lives; about half of that amount is spent in the final two months of life. The elderly patient spends an average of $5,200 on end-of-life care for him or herself, and private insurance pays about 5 percent of the costs. Despite cost-cutting measures, end-of-life costs represented about 25 percent of total Medicare expenditures over the past 25 years.

According to a Rand Health white paper, *Adapting Health Care to Serious Chronic Illness in Old Age,* how Americans live and die changed dramatically in the 20th century. Not only do people live substantially longer today than they did a hundred years ago, but they also take longer to die. In the past, the time from the onset of a serious disease to death may have been as little as two weeks. Today, people may live as long as two to three years beyond the onset of a terminal illness. In the past, the dying were cared for almost exclu-

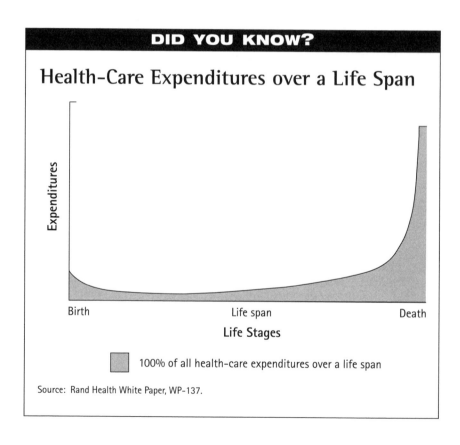

DID YOU KNOW?

Health-Care Expenditures over a Life Span

100% of all health-care expenditures over a life span

Source: Rand Health White Paper, WP-137.

sively at home; today about half of the people who die in a given year—about 55,000 people—die in hospitals. Because people live longer with chronic illnesses and tend to require hospitalization, health-care costs tend to be highest at the end of life. In the past those costs were distributed more evenly throughout the life span.

Many people assume that because 25 percent of all Medicare expenditures are incurred during the final year of life that the elderly receive expensive and painful, but futile, treatments. When they think about an old woman dying in the hospital, they picture her connected to high-tech machines and subjected to a wide variety of medical procedures. According to *Seven Deadly Myths: Uncovering the Facts about the High Cost of the Last Year of Life,* published by the Alliance for Aging Research, that picture is largely false. A 1993 study published in the *New England Journal of Medicine* entitled "Trends in Medicare Payments in the Last Year of Life" demonstrates that only about 3 percent of all Medicare patients received costly aggressive treatment (such as surgery, dialysis, or heart catheterization) at the end of life. According to a Congressional Research Service study, "analysis of expenditure patterns lends little support to the assertion that high-technology medical care for the terminally ill contributes disproportionately to expenditures for those who die or to the argument that overall spending at the end of life is inordinately high and could be reduced."

The Alliance for Aging Research concluded, "These findings suggest that physicians and hospitals are not blindly ordering heroic measures to prolong dying, despite the popular misconception." Thus, although health-care costs at the end of life are high, they are not, apparently, artificially inflated by inappropriate care.

In 1982 a benefit was added to Medicare to provide hospice care for patients with fewer than six months to live. A hospice is a facility or service that provides supportive care for the terminally ill and their families. One of the reasons for the addition of this benefit is that hospice care is less expensive than hospital care for many terminally ill patients. According to the Hospice Association of America, a day in a hospital costs approximately $2,000, compared to $500 for a day in a skilled nursing facility and $113 for a day of hospice care.

The General Accounting Office of the U.S. government has found that the Medicare hospice benefit is not used as much as the government expected. Medicare patients stay in hospice for an average of only 19 days out of the six months that they are entitled to, and only 19 percent of dying patients enter a hospice. Some researchers speculate that patients and their families do not use the hospice benefit because they do not want to admit that the patient is terminally ill.

Q & A

Question: What is the cost to the American economy of the care family members provide to parents and other relatives during their last year of life?

Answer: According to the U.S. Department of Health and Human Services, "employees who are also caregivers cost U.S. employers $29 billion annually, which translates into an annual cost of $1,142.50 per employee. Costs are a result of absenteeism, partial absenteeism, coming in late, and leaving early." According to "Medicare Facts and Faces," informal caregivers provide about $196 billion in uncompensated care annually. Also according to "Medicare Facts and Faces," taking time away from work to care for an ailing relative can cost the caregiver as much as $650,000 in lost wages, Social Security, and pension contributions.

FUNERAL EXPENSES

In 1963, British writer Jessica Mitford published *The American Way of Death,* an exposé of the greedy and unethical practices of some funeral professionals. The book was incredibly popular, with its first edition selling out within just one day. *The American Way of Death* prompted the Federal Trade Commission (FTC) to adopt new regulations that limited some of the worst practices of the funeral industry.

Mitford showed in her book how funeral professionals were trained to exploit the grief of surviving relatives by encouraging them to spend huge amounts of money on unnecessary procedures and fancy extras. She quoted an article from a trade journal, for example, advising funeral directors to urge family members to "atone for any real or fancied neglect of the deceased" by buying the most expensive casket possible.

Today, the FTC forbids the following practices, which were common when Mitford wrote her exposé:

- Claiming that embalming is required by law
- Showing the grieving family only the most expensive caskets

- Claiming that some caskets can prevent the decomposition of the body
- Hiding charges and overcharging
- Claiming that caskets are required for cremation by law

Jessica Mitford died in 1996; she spent the years before her death revising *The American Way of Death* and the new edition, *The American Way of Death Revisited,* was published in 1998. Mitford was no less critical of the funeral industry in this book than in her earlier one. She noted that the industry has managed to find ways around many of the laws designed to rein in greedy practices and lamented changes that have resulted in skyrocketing funeral costs, including multinational corporations buying up family-run funeral homes.

What do funerals cost? The average price tag for a funeral in the United States today, according to the FTC, is $6,000, and many funerals end up costing $10,000 or more. The costs for a typical funeral (costing a little over $7,000) may be broken down as follows:

- Professional services (including embalming and charges for funeral home staff): $1,650
- Facilities and equipment (including visitation room, preparation room, etc.): $850
- Transportation (from the place of death and limos for the funeral service): $450
- Merchandise (casket, prayer cards, etc.): $2,515
- Cash expenses (obituary, flowers, death certificate, cemetery plot): $1,828

The list of costs does not include the actual cost of the burial (the opening and closing the grave), which can add from $400 to $600 to the total cost. Clearly, the casket is among the most expensive elements of a funeral. While the average amount paid for a casket is about $2,000, mahogany or bronze caskets can cost more than $10,000. Many consumers have saved money by buying caskets from wholesalers rather than a funeral home. Funeral homes typically mark up the price of a casket from 300 to 500 percent. In the past, many funeral homes would tell family members that they had to buy the casket from them in order to use their services, but this practice is no longer legal.

WILLS AND ESTATE TAXES

Because most people do not like to think about their own deaths, many put off making a will, a legal document declaring a person's wishes regarding the disposal of his or her property after death. A person who dies without a will is said to have died intestate. When a person dies intestate, the state in which the deceased person lived determines how his or her assets will be distributed. For some families, how the government distributes assets will be similar to what the deceased may have wanted; for other families, dying intestate can be a disaster. For example, if a man dies intestate in New Jersey leaving a wife and two minor children, his estate will be distributed as follows:

- His wife receives the first $50,000 plus half of the remaining total.
- The children receive the remaining amount in equal shares.

The man in the example may have planned for his wife to inherit the entire estate, so that she would have enough to live on and support their children. But in the absence of a will, half of the estate minus $50,000 will be held in trust for the children until they reach the age of 18. If a person dies intestate with no heirs, as defined by state laws, the state will claim the entire estate.

Few Americans need to worry about paying an estate tax, or the so-called death tax. In 2004, only those who inherited an estate worth more than $1.5 million needed to pay the tax. By 2009, people will be able to leave up to $3.5 million without incurring a tax liability. However, for those who have family businesses, the estate tax can be devastating, with 18 to 55 cents on every dollar over $1.5 million going to the government. In many cases, people have had to sell family businesses to pay the tax. According to Pennsylvania senator Rick Santorum, 70 percent of family businesses do not survive the first generation of ownership and 87 percent do not survive the second generation because of the tax.

See also: Cremation; Death and Dying, The Business of

FURTHER READING
Mitford, Jessica. *The American Way of Death Revisited.* Reprint, New York: Vintage, 2000.

■ DEATH AND THE FAMILY

Social scientist Kathleen Gilbert of Indiana University, in her 2001 article "We've Had the Same Loss, Why Don't We Have the Same Grief?: Family Meanings and Family Grief," emphasizes that while grief affects families, families themselves do not grieve. Grieving is an individual process that takes place within the context of the family. According to the General Social Survey (GSS), 36 million Americans deal with the death of a family member each year, and families may be disrupted for as long as three years as its members try to cope with the loss.

FAMILIES AS SYSTEMS

A family is a system, meaning that its members are organized in a whole that is more than the sum of its parts. Professor Gilbert suggests that taking this approach considers the way relationships within the family and among family members, as well as the relationship between the family and other elements of the social environment, influence the response to loss by individuals and by the family as a whole. As with all systems, families strive for stability (they want things to stay the same) and yet must be flexible enough to deal with changes when they come.

Death affects the family system in a variety of ways. When a family member dies, the "wholeness" of the family is broken, at least temporarily, and the family has to reconstitute itself, to become whole again without the missing relative. Roles that family members have typically played may be disrupted. For example, when a woman loses her husband, she may expect or need the protection of an older son or she may become dependent on one or more of her children for emotional support. Children who had few responsibilities may suddenly find that they have new and unwelcome burdens.

Roles other than those that describe a person's place in the family structure (mother, daughter, brother) may also be affected. A sister who was always considered the "strong one" in the family may be overwhelmed by grief, while another sibling, always the family "peacemaker," suddenly seems to be in conflict with everyone.

A major problem that affects families as they grieve is that every person reacts differently to a loss. According to Gilbert, "each family member makes certain assumptions about others in the family, one of which may be that because they have lost the same individual, their grief should be the same." Family members, however, seldom express grief in identical ways. Some of the factors that affect reactions to a loss include:

- The nature of the relationship between a family member and the deceased, particularly whether it was a close relationship or a distant one
- Whether there were unresolved conflicts between the deceased and the family member
- How each family member regards the loss (for some the loss may be devastating; for others—such as caregivers for people with Alzheimer's or other dementias—a relief)
- Whether the death was anticipated and prepared for, or sudden and traumatic

Clinical psychologist Therese Rando, writing in "Grief, Dying, and Death: Clinical Interventions for Caregivers" (1984), emphasizes even more potential differences among family members. She writes, "Each family is a collection of individuals. Reactions . . . will be affected by variables such as personality, coping abilities, age and maturity, gender, relationship with the person, intelligence, education, mental and physical health, religion and philosophy, fears, knowledge and experiences with illness [and] formal and informal supports." Not only do family members differ in all of these ways but they may also have different grieving styles. One person may want to tell funny stories about the relative, while another may feel that laughter is inappropriate or disrespectful.

Adult siblings who lose a parent may find that childhood rivalries return. Instead of supporting one another in their loss, brothers and sisters may fight over who mom "loved best." In fact, according to sociologists Larry Peppers and Ronald Knapp in *Motherhood and Mourning* (1980), family members frequently experience conflicting forms and levels of grief. Moreover, as sociologist Paul Rosenblatt's research reveals in "Difficulties in Supporting the Bereaved" (1991), grieving family members in need of support are the *least* likely to get it from one another and are better off depending on friends for such assistance.

The irony, of course, is that just when family members think they will pull together and support one another in their mutual loss, they may find they are fighting and criticizing one another, adding more stress to an already stressful situation. As Gilbert notes, "the drive for a shared family view [of the loss] is powerful and a lack of one is painful for family members. Logically, the push should be for consistency. Yet, trying to establish a single view may be counterproductive [and] it may be best to recognize that there are aspects of the loss that are open to discussion and confirmation within the family and others that are not."

THE MANY FACES OF FAMILY LOSS

Many people claim that the death of a child is the most difficult loss anyone can experience. Parents are likely to feel not only grief but also guilt for their failure to protect the child. For example, parents who have lost a baby to sudden infant death syndrome (SIDS) experience profound and often debilitating guilt. Sometimes parents idealize the child who died, causing other children in the family to feel inadequate and unloved. Mothers and fathers often grieve in sharply different ways, causing stress on the marriage.

In 1977, Harriet Schiff, herself a bereaved parent, estimated that as many as 75 percent of marriages do not survive the death of a child. Her estimate was a guess that she used primarily to encourage scholars to research the question. Unfortunately, many people, including psychologists and grief counselors, took Schiff's number as valid. A recent study by sociology professor Mark Hardt suggests that most marriages do survive the death of a child, with only about 9 percent ending in divorce as a direct result of the death. It may be significant that most of those who responded to Hardt's survey said they had sought professional counseling after the child's death.

Fact Or Fiction?

Women who miscarry do not really grieve for the loss of the child, since they have never really known the child.

Fact: Obstetrician Ashley Hill has found that most women who have had a miscarriage have heard unbelievably insensitive comments from their friends and family. In some cases this has led to permanently damaged relationships. Comments such as "the baby would have been deformed anyway," "it must be punishment for something you did wrong," or even "you can always have more" can be extremely painful to a woman and her partner. A similarly disturbing comment is "how can you be so upset—you were barely pregnant."

Women and their partners who suffer a miscarriage often experience severe grief over the loss of their baby. It does not matter how far along the mother was at the time of her loss; in fact, many women grieve as much over the loss of a baby in the first trimester as they do for a still-born baby or a baby who dies many months or years after birth. Grief is individual, and friends and loved ones should try to be supportive through this difficult process.

Young children grieve when they lose a parent, but they may also experience confusion because they do not really understand death, fear that others they love will die, and feel a profound sense of abandonment. According to the American Academy of Child and Adolescent Psychiatry, young children may become angry, have nightmares, or regress into infantile behavior, such as bed-wetting. Some may even believe that they caused the death of the parent because they were angry with the parent at one time or other. According to *Working with Bereaved Children: A Guide,* produced by the Children's Legal Centre, Colchester, United Kingdom, and the Institute of Special Pedagogics and Psychology, St. Petersburg, Russia, in 2004, an adolescent who loses a parent may have trouble coping with the intensity of his or her feelings and "may display risk taking behavior, using drugs, alcohol and self harming as a way of gaining control or dealing with their grief."

The loss of a husband or wife brings its own set of difficulties, especially if the couple had very young children. Grief may be complicated by financial difficulties and having to learn to do tasks that had been performed by the deceased spouse. If the children are grown or the couple never had children, the surviving spouse may feel intense loneliness. Since 85 percent of women outlive their husbands, many of the people who lose a spouse are women who may experience isolation because the couple's married friends exclude her from social functions.

According to T.J. Wray, a professor of religious studies and the author of *Living through Grief When an Adult Brother or Sister Dies* (2003), losing a brother or sister can be an especially painful experience: "In terms of the span of time, the intimacy, and the shared experience of childhood, no other relationship rivals the connection we have with our adult brothers or sisters." Only brothers and sisters know firsthand what it was like to grow up as a child in a particular family. According to "Experiencing the Death of a Sibling as a Child," published by the Sibling Connection, children who experience the loss of a brother or sister frequently compensate by becoming overprotective parents. The death of a twin can be especially difficult; the surviving twin often reports a sense of having lost a part of him or herself. According to psychotherapist Joan Woodward, who founded a support group called the Lone Twin Network, "If you ask me what is the difference between losing a twin and losing a sister or a brother, I can only answer that . . . the loss of a co-twin seems to make us aware that we have lost a person who ought to be with us all the time. So without belittling the loss of a sister or brother, because I know full well that this can be hard enough for some people, the fundamental difference seems to be that twins have been together from the very moment of conception."

HOW FAMILIES RESOLVE GRIEF

Psychologist John R. Jordan says to resolve grief at the loss of a loved one, a family must carry out three important tasks. First, the family has to recognize and acknowledge the loss felt by each member. Secondly, it has to reorganize itself. And, finally, the family has to learn to accept the new organization. Most psychologists and bereavement researchers agree that open and honest communication is essential for healing.

According to Gilbert, "Supportive communication facilitates discussion of thoughts and emotions and makes it easier for members to share their beliefs about the loss and its meanings for them. One important element of the communication process and one that cannot be overlooked is that family members must engage in the simple but difficult act of listening to each other." It is also extremely important for family members to accept differences in grieving style, to try to focus on what similarities there are, and to reframe the differences as strengths.

See also: Attitudes Toward Death, Teenage; Death of a Parent; Grieving, The Process of

FURTHER READING
Becvar, Dorothy Stroh. *In the Presence of Grief: Helping Family Members Resolve Death, Dying, and Bereavement Issues.* New York: Guilford Press, 2001.

Rosen, Elliott J. *Families Facing Death: Family Dynamics of Terminal Illness.* Lanham, MD: Lexington Books, 1990.

■ DEATH OF A FRIEND

Most of the literature on grieving focuses on the death of a close family member. Much less has been written on how people react to the death of a friend. According to Leona Doyle Lane, in her graduate thesis, "When a Good Friend Dies: Four Adolescents' Experience with Grief," (University of New Brunswick, Canada, 2001), "the loss of an adolescent's close friend is generally overlooked in the literature and in society." There is some research, according to Lane, on how teenagers react to the loss of a peer but not much on how they react to the death of a close friend. Lane adds that it is likely that, "Grief as experienced by adolescents is a different and unique experience that needs to be studied as a separate phenomenon." Because close friendships are such a significant part of adolescent development, this lack of research is somewhat surprising.

As adolescents become more and more independent of their parents, their relationship with peers becomes increasingly important. Because adolescence is a critical developmental stage, unresolved grief over a death—a close family member or a friend—can spell problems for the future. Lane notes, "Adolescents develop many new ways to comprehend the world. With integrative abilities, adolescent are able to formulate a strong sense of who they are (ego identity) and where they are headed. . . . Adolescents' identity shifts away from parents toward friends as they increasingly see themselves as members of their peer culture. . . The loss of a peer can upset an identity formation that may already be unstable." In a 1995 study, "Beyond the Innocence of Childhood," D. W. Adams and E. J. Deveau noted that developmental needs of teens can be profoundly affected by the death of a close friend. Lane adds that "the loss of a close friend may indeed influence adolescents at a very deep emotional level."

A number of factors can complicate grieving for an adolescent who has lost a friend. Adolescents who are grieving may need to talk over their feelings with their parents and other adults, but, because they are so focused on demonstrating their own independence, they may not ask for help. This ambivalence, according to Lane, "creates a tug-of-war between the need to be independent and the need for parents as a safe haven."

Adolescents may also be disappointed by the reaction of their peers. While they may expect peers to be sympathetic, teens typically do not know how to react to grief and may avoid the grieving person out of fear and embarrassment, leaving the teen who has lost a friend to cope with feelings of loneliness as well as grief. And because adolescence is an emotional time anyway, teens may experience overwhelmingly intense emotions when a friend dies. Also, according to V. E. Kandt in his 1994 article "Adolescent Bereavement: Turning a Fragile Time into Acceptance and Peace," grieving adolescents may move quickly back and forth among the various stages of grief (denial, anger, bargaining, depression, acceptance), and it may take a long time, perhaps as long as two years, before they can accept the death of a close friend. Because adolescents are still developing and have other life stages to travel through, they may need to revisit the death over and over, gradually accepting the loss as they mature. Another factor that can complicate teens' grieving is the fact that a friend's death, more than that of a parent or sibling, sometimes causes the surviving adolescent to consider his or her own eventual death, according to Lane. Thus the grieving teen is actually mourning the loss of his or her sense of immortality as well as the loss of a friend. Finally, because the chief causes of death among adolescents are unintentional injuries, suicide, and homicide, it is likely that an adolescent who loses a friend will have little or no time to prepare for the death and may have to deal with violent imagery when reimagining the circumstances of the death.

TEENS SPEAK

I Lost My Best Friend

I'm in a support group with other kids like me who have lost a friend in a car crash, and I'm just realizing how special Carl's parents are. In talking to the other kids in the group, I learned that many of them felt that no one understood how much they cared about their friend, so they felt they really couldn't express their grief. Everyone consoled the family members, but no one seemed to think that friends were hurting just as much. When Carl died, his parents made me part of the family. They introduced me to everyone as "Carl's best friend" and asked me to speak at the services. And afterward, they let me go through Carl's things and choose something to remember him by. Their kindness really helped me to come to terms with Carl's death. I think I'm going to visit Mr. and Mrs. Iverson this week and thank them for all the things they did for me, when they were hurting so much themselves.

WHAT IS A FRIEND?

Another complicating factor when a friend dies—and this is true for adults as well as teenagers—is the fact that the word "friend" suggests many different kinds of relationships of many differing intensities. "Friend" may refer to a companion from youth whom one has not seen in 20 years, to a new, casual acquaintance, or to a soul mate. This may make the loss of a friend an ambiguous loss in that people may make incorrect assumptions about the nature of what the grieving person is feeling. If a person says, "My father died" or "My daughter died" or "My brother died," most listeners will be able to make a fairly good estimate of the degree of loss and respond appropriately. But if a person says "My friend died," the nature of the loss is not necessarily clear. The truth of the matter is that young people are sometimes closer to their friends than to family, and the loss of a friend may be much more devastating than the loss of a family member. Yet people other than the one who has experienced the loss may have no idea about the intensity of the feelings. This situation may lead to what grief researchers call "disenfranchised grief."

According to Kathleen R. Gilbert in her 2004 article "Grief in a Family Context," "Disenfranchised grief is the result of a loss for which [people] do not have a socially recognized right, role or capacity to grieve. Those socially ambiguous losses are not or cannot be openly mourned, or socially supported. Essentially, this is grief that is restricted by 'grieving rules' ascribed by the culture and society. The bereaved may not publicly grieve because, somehow, some element or elements of the loss prevent a public recognition."

Thus, a teenager who loses a dear friend may not be recognized as suffering a loss as great as or greater than family members and may not receive expressions of sorrow or concern, or may even be told to "get over it," because others do not think the grief is appropriate. Disenfranchised grief can make the emotional reaction to the death much harder to deal with. According to Gilbert, disenfranchised grief intensifies feelings of anger, guilt, and powerlessness and results in a more complicated grief response. "Rituals may be absent or the grievers may be excluded from rituals. The reduced or absent social support promotes a sense of generalized isolation on the part of the griever."

Q & A

Question: What are some typical situations in which people may experience ambiguous loss and disenfranchised grief?

Answer: Besides the loss of a friend, there are a number of situations in which people may be expected not to feel much grief. Losing a child to miscarriage and stillbirth are particularly difficult in that mothers may feel as strongly as those who have lost an older child. Losing a homosexual partner can also be very problematic, especially if the blood relatives of the person who has died refuse to acknowledge the relationship. The death of an ex-spouse or a stepparent may not be recognized by others as painful. Losing a very elderly relative can also create problems if people expect the survivors not to be bothered because the person was so old.

COPING WITH THE DEATH OF A FRIEND

According to Leona Doyle Lane, several factors influence the ability of adolescents to cope with the death of a friend. Her study revealed that the support of peers is extremely important, especially in allowing a teen to take his or her mind off the death for a time. A teen's friends were a key factor in helping survivors cope. However, it was also ambiguous. The teen's friends did not necessarily discuss the death of the friend and may have focused little on the person's death. In fact, the teen's friends were trying to get their minds off the death. Grieving teens in this study felt that their friends did not understand their grief, and some reported comments suggesting that they did not have a right to their intense feelings. Despite this, however, the comfort offered by peers was regarded as important by teens in this study.

The support of parents was also important but less crucial for these teens than the support of peers. While some of the teens in the study confided in their mothers—fathers were seldom mentioned—they seemed primarily to feel that parents helped by "being there" and understanding their need to be with peers.

Lane noted, "Researchers in other studies have found that one can maintain a healthy ongoing attachment with a deceased loved one." The teenagers in Lane's study also felt that their friend was still present to them in some way—could perhaps even see and hear them—and this provided comfort.

Teenagers who are grieving the death of a friend need, first and foremost, for the people around them to recognize the legitimacy of their grief and the depth of their feelings. They need the support of peers, who will listen to them and also provide distractions. They need the understanding of their parents as they seek solace from their peers. And they need to feel that the friend is still, in some way, part of their lives. These factors can help prevent complicated grief and the need for therapy to recover.

See also: Attitudes Toward Death, Teenage; Death and the Family; Death of a Parent; Grieving, The Process of; Loss of a Pet; Teenage Deaths

FURTHER READING
Smith, Harold Ivan. *Grieving the Death of a Friend.* Minneapolis, MN: Augsburg Fortress Publishers, 1996.

■ DEATH OF A PARENT

When a parent dies, the central loss may be accompanied by a series of what psychologists call secondary losses. Parents exert a powerful influence on children. From the moment of birth, they contribute immeasurably to the development of a child's personality and sense of self. They offer help, support, and unconditional love. They represent a child's sense of safety and security. When a parent dies, then, children—of any age—may feel that they have lost much more than a parent. They may feel that the world is no longer a safe place to be; they may feel that they will never be truly loved again; they may feel that important links to their childhood are gone forever; and they may feel that they have lost the only thing that separated them from their own mortality. Thus the death of a parent can have profound and lasting effects on a person, creating an emptiness that is hard to fill.

WHEN CHILDREN LOSE A PARENT

According to the U.S. Census Bureau, approximately 2 percent of children will lose a parent before they reach their 18th birthday. Children of different ages will react differently to the death of a parent, but children of every age are deeply affected. Even infants and babies react to the loss of a parent, especially to the loss of a mother. According to Donna Schuurman, director of the Dougy Center for Grieving Children and Families, in her book *Never the Same: Coming to Terms with the Death of a Parent* (2003), even an infant can "instinctively sense" the absence of the mother. Because the central developmental task of infancy is to learn to trust that he or she will be safe and protected, the death of a mother may interfere with the child's sense of security as it develops.

Older children, up to the age of six, are struggling to develop independence and initiative. They are taking their first steps away from parents, and the shock of a death may sometimes cause a regression in behavior. For example, a child who is toilet trained may wet the bed. Because children of this age think they are the "center of the universe," according to Schuurman, they may believe that something they did caused the parent's death or that they might have done something to prevent it. Children in this stage of development do not understand that death is permanent and may ask when the parent is coming back.

Preadolescent children go through a developmental stage that psychologist Erik Erikson called "industry." From the ages of six to 12, children learn new tasks and begin to compare their performance to that of other children. The death of a parent at this stage may lead to "paralysis in . . . development." Children may find that they cannot concentrate on schoolwork and may experience sleep problems and headaches. As with younger children, they may also believe that something they did caused the death.

Adolescents ages 13 and older are trying to define themselves as individuals and to explore their differences from their parents. Often this differentiation involves discovering that one's parents are ordinary human beings with all sorts of faults and quirks. It may also involve frequent clashes and arguments. Thus, when a parent dies, there may be unresolved issues in the relationship that make grieving the death even harder. Because adolescents have reached the stage of cognitive development in which they can understand abstract concepts, the death of a parent is likely to lead to a realization of their own mortality. Psychologists note that when a child loses a parent, that loss must be "reprocessed" through each stage of life, so that it is almost as if the loss keeps repeating itself. While a three-year-old girl might miss her daddy, when that same girl is ready to graduate from high school, she may grieve all over again because her father will not be there to see her graduate.

In *Never the Same*, Schuurman also points out that many adults do not know how to help a child deal with the death of a parent. They may exclude children from funeral preparations, may discourage them from showing emotion, and may tell them that they are now "the man" or "the woman" of the house. Consequently, children who lose a parent before the age of 18 may grow up with a number of unresolved issues that affect all areas of their lives.

According to Schuurman, studies have consistently shown seven key differences between children who lost a parent and those who did not. Bereaved children are:

- More likely to suffer from depression
- More likely to have health problems and be accident-prone
- Significantly more likely to perform poorly in school
- Significantly more prone to anxiety and fear
- More likely to believe that they cannot control what happens to them
- Significantly more pessimistic

Clearly, not every child who loses a parent fits this pattern. Schuurman identifies three factors that seem to protect children from the ravages of unresolved grief. One is the child's "internal makeup." A child who is affectionate and easygoing, possesses good reasoning skills and a positive self-image, and believes that he or she is in control of what happens and may be less likely to suffer from unresolved grief. A second protective factor is the nature of the immediate family. A child who is surrounded by a family in which "truth, commitment, hope, optimism, a sense of control, and a sense of meaning" are part of the home environment is more likely to do well following the death of a parent. The third protective factor is the ability of the child to find support from outside the family.

Schuurman also identifies three behaviors that can help children cope with the death of a parent and avoid permanent scars. One is to "maintain psychological contact with [the] deceased parent." This might include writing letters to the parent, wearing an article of their clothing or jewelry, or carrying on imaginary conversations with the parent. The second behavior is to maintain "a changing mental relationship" with the parent. As the child grows, that is, the memory of the parent grows also. Thus, a little boy who thought his daddy was the strongest man in the world must, as he matures, come to understand and remember his father as a real person, with weaknesses and faults, and not as a superman. The third behavior is to alternate grieving with getting on with life and not to do one or the other to excess.

TEENS SPEAK

Wearing Her Dad's Tie Helped My Friend Annie

My friend Annie lost her dad to a brain tumor last year. It was really awful—Annie's in a lot of plays, and she was on stage when her dad died. Her mom was waiting to tell her backstage. Even though she knew it was coming, Annie was devastated. She didn't come back to school for almost two weeks, but when she did she was wearing one of her dad's ties. I asked her what was up, and she said she decided that she would wear one of her dad's ties every day until graduation, as a way of staying close to him. At first people stared at her and gave her weird looks. But after a while they got used to it, and most people even thought it was a pretty good idea. I think it helped Annie deal with what had happened—really, it's kind of sweet.

WHEN ADULTS LOSE A PARENT

According to Debra Umberson, author of *Death of a Parent: Transition to a New Adult Identity* (2003), "The death of a parent is the most common cause of bereavement faced by adults in Western society. Each year about 5 percent of the U.S. population is faced with this experience. Only one in 10 adults has lost a parent by age 25, but by age 54, 50 percent of adults have lost both parents, and by age 62, 75 percent have lost both parents. Despite the fact that people are aware that they will lose their elderly parents, many adults suffer a tremendous sense of loss when their parents die.

The death of a parent imposes an unexpected crisis for most healthy, well-functioning adults. This crisis can result in high levels of psychological distress, increased risk for depression, impaired physical health, or increased alcohol consumption. These effects go largely unrecognized by everyone except those going through the loss, and the bereaved often assume that they are unusual in their strong response to the loss. Umberson adds that the death of a parent initiates a period of self-reflection and the transformation of adult identity.

The transformation may be positive or negative, depending on the nature of the relationship between the adult child and the parent and on the nature of the support systems available to the grieving adult. Umberson finds, for example, that the death of a parent has a negative effect on many marriages. Women, in particular, feel hurt by their husbands' lack of empathy. On the other hand, when an adult loses a parent, he or she may feel a strong concern for and interest in the next generations. When their parents die, many adults begin to wonder how their own children will remember them and they begin to think about what sort of **legacy** they will leave. Others look for and find reminders of the deceased parent in one or more children. Thus, unlike marital relationships, relationships with children are likely to improve after an adult loses a parent.

Q & A

Question: How does the death of a parent affect the relationships of brothers and sisters?

Answer: In some families, siblings grow closer, and in some families, the death of the parent leads to conflict and anger. One of the problems is the belief that because they lost the same person, brothers and sisters will have the same reaction to the death. However, parents have different relationships with each of their children, leading siblings to react quite differently. In the emotional time that follows a death, differences in grieving behavior may lead to quarrels. Siblings may also fight over who gets what, especially after the only remaining parent dies.

Often, after a parent's death, adults make deliberate changes to be more like that parent or to become the sort of person the parent would have wanted. These changes can be very positive and affirming for some people. On the other hand, Umberson says, adult children of abusive or alcoholic parents may find themselves following along the same path after the parent's death, even if they hated the parent's behavior during that person's life. Other adults, if they had a critical or unloving parent, may find themselves relieved by the death and able to make very positive changes in their lives. Ultimately, says Umberson, "The relationship between parent and child continues throughout our lives, even after our parent dies. The death of a parent is a powerful, transformative moment in the ebb and flow of life. From this painful loss can emerge transcendence to a new adult identity."

See also: Death and the Family; Death of a Friend; Loss of a Pet; Teenage Deaths

FURTHER READING

Schuurman, Donna. *Never the Same: Coming to Terms with the Death of a Parent.* New York: St. Martin's Press, 2003.
Umberson, Debra. *Death of a Parent: Transition to a New Adult Identity.* Cambridge: Cambridge University Press, 2003.

■ DOCTORS' PERSPECTIVES

During a 2001 panel discussion at the annual Association for Death Education and Counseling in Toronto, Canada, cardiologist Lofty Basta stated that most doctors do not do a very good job in caring for dying patients. He said that doctors seldom talk about dying, acting as though death should not happen.

Theologian Stanley Hauerwas, in his 2000 book *Naming the Silences: God, Medicine, and the Problem of Suffering,* presents the problem more bluntly: Curing, not caring, has become medicine's primary purpose, and physicians have become warriors engaged in a combat with death. What Hauerwas is referring to is the fact that medical training emphasizes how to keep patients alive, rather than helping them, if need be, to die as comfortably as possible. This attitude sometimes causes doctors to resort to "extraordinary means," such as feeding tubes and ventilators, to keep people alive, even if such devices diminish the quality of the dying patient's final days.

In the Missoula Demonstration Project, a 15-year study exploring issues of death and dying, Ira Byock, a physician, writes that hospital-based care of dying people often ignores the patients' preferences for refusing futile life-prolonging care. Commonly accepted medical practice inadequately treats and in fact inadequately addresses dying people's discomfort. Hospitals isolate terminal patients from their families. Byock predicts that without substantial changes in doctors' attitudes "most of us will die in an intensive care unit surrounded by machines, violated by tubes, having all kinds of intervention, while existing in perhaps a mindless or unconscious state, connected to a disabled body that will never recover."

Like most people, doctors experience anxiety when they confront the idea of death. They do not like to be reminded of their own mortality, and they do not like to feel helpless. According to a 1990 article published in the *Family Practice Research Journal,* younger doctors and those who had little training in medical school about how to deal with death were the most uncomfortable around dying patients. Older, more experienced doctors and those with strong religious beliefs were more at ease with the subject.

A doctor who is uncomfortable around death may fail to communicate clearly with patients, may prescribe unnecessary treatments, or may fail to provide adequate **palliative care,** care that does not attempt to cure but rather allows the patient to be comfortable, alert, and pain-free in his or her final weeks or months. Some doctors fear giving enough pain medication to make the patient comfortable for fear of legal action against them, because the medication, while freeing the patient of pain, may also hasten death. In other cases, doctors withdraw emotionally, leaving dying patients feeling abandoned just as they may desperately need a sense of connectedness.

Educating doctors about death and dying

Fortunately, many medical schools have begun to realize the importance of training doctors to deal with dying patients. A 1998 study by the Association of American Medical Colleges reports that 96 percent of medical schools now discuss death and dying, though just a few schools actually devote an entire course to the subject. A 2001 article by Amy Dicresce in *Wayne Medicine* details just such a program at Wayne State University School of Medicine, in Detroit, Michigan. There, third-year students spend time in a **hospice**, a facility where dying patients spend their final days in a homelike atmosphere with adequate pain management. Often students are amazed at how happy hospice patients are; they are not in pain, they have accepted the fact of their own mortality, and they can spend the time they have left enjoying life and interactions with their families.

John Finn, executive medical director of Hospice of Michigan, says that many doctors today are not aware of some of the options available to people who are dying, and many do not know how to ease suffering. Wayne State hopes its program will ensure that its graduates are more aware of these issues.

The medical school at the University of Rochester, in New York, offers a course entitled "Improving Communication at the End of Life." One of the presenters of the course, Timothy Quill, says that most physicians feel unprepared to provide competent care to dying patients or even to participate in decisions at the end of life. He explains that most physicians avoid talking about death-related issues with their patients. As a result, the patient's care and medical decisions become driven by technology rather than thoughtful discussions between doctor, patient, and family. Poor communication holds doctors back from delivering quality care at the end of life. The course also covers how to tell a patient that he or she is dying, how important it is for patients to be able to say good-bye to their families, how to communicate important facts about pain management, and how to help patients continue to hope for a good death even if a cure is not possible.

A 1999 study published in the *Journal of Residency Education* looked at what attitudes and personal characteristics might influence doctors' attitudes toward death. The authors of the study found a link between a doctor's ability to tolerate uncertainty and his or her attitude toward dying patients. Doctors who were uncertain about how to help dying patients had more negative feelings about dealing with the dying than those who were more certain. And doctors who did not want to admit they were uncertain had even more negative attitudes. The authors concluded that there is a need for clear practice guidelines for making the transition to palliative care to be part of medical training programs. They also noted that 44 percent of medical students had never been present when an attending physician talked with a dying patient and recommended that medical faculty model such communications, including the expression of uncertainty, for medical students.

Euthanasia and physician-assisted suicide

In physician–assisted suicide (PAS), a physician helps a terminally ill person who is mentally competent experience a peaceful, painless death. PAS is controversial because physicians are trained to preserve life—not end it. Those for and against PAS disagree on several controversial issues: self-determination, relief of suffering, and killing versus allowing to die.

Q & A

Question: Does the Hippocratic oath—which most doctors take upon graduation from medical school—forbid physician-assisted suicide?

Answer: The Hippocratic Oath has undergone a number of changes since it was first developed in ancient Greece. The original version does prohibit physician-assisted suicide, requiring the doctor to pledge, "I will neither give a deadly drug to anybody who asked for it, nor will I make a suggestion to this effect."

The oath, however, has been modified many times over the years in order to adapt to changing values and ideas. According to a 1993 survey of U.S. and Canadian medical schools, only 14 percent of modern oaths prohibit euthanasia.

Because self-determination is so highly valued in the U.S. legal tradition, attempts to justify PAS usually start with an appeal to this principle. Proponents argue that a decision to end life is a personal issue and that no one other than the individual person is qualified to decide. Opponents argue that self-determinism is not sufficient to justify taking a life, especially by a physician.

Relief of suffering is also a contentious point. Although many doctors have had patients for whom death would seem to be a relief, few believe that the way to deal with suffering is to do away with the sufferer. Others, however, believe that it is a physician's duty to relieve suffering, and that if suffering cannot be relieved with medication, doctors ought to consider helping a competent person who is in pain to end his or her life.

The third area of controversy is the distinction between active **euthanasia**, or causing someone to die who no longer desires to live, and passive euthanasia, which, for example, may allow someone to die by removing a feeding tube. Proponents of active euthanasia argue that there is no important moral distinction between the two practices and that because passive euthanasia is allowed in the United States, the active form should be allowed too. Opponents argue that the two practices are fundamentally different. They note that when life support is withdrawn, the cause of death is the underlying disease, not the actions of the physician. Such is not the case in active euthanasia, where the doctor may assist the patient to die by deliberately administering an overdose of a pain medication. In such a case, the cause of death is the medication.

There are only two places in the world where active euthanasia is legal: the Netherlands and the state of Oregon, which passed legislation legalizing physician-assisted suicide in 1994. Interestingly, since the practice was legalized, doctors say they are not more likely to assist with suicide but more frequently refer patients to hospice care and have tried to learn more about the use of pain medication to treat terminally ill patients. A 2001 article published in the *Journal of the American Medical Association* by Linda Ganzini concludes that care for terminally ill patients in Oregon has improved since 1994.

For many years, medical practice and training concentrated on curing patients but offered neither insight nor guidance on handling circumstances where a cure was impossible. While some doctor-patient interactions at the end of life raise ethical questions, medical schools and medical professionals have begun to address the question of the terminal patient as more than merely a matter of technology.

See also: Right to Die, The

FURTHER READING
Parker, E. *Life Is a Gift*. Fort Bragg, CA: Lost Coast Press, 2003.

■ DRUG AND ALCOHOL ABUSE

Excessive use of drugs or alcohol in order to evoke a feeling or emotion (to "get high") or because one is physically or psychologically dependent on the substance is abuse. The exact definition of abuse differs depending on whether the substance in question is legal or illegal and, sometimes, on the age of the abuser. In the case of alcohol, for example, an adult is said to have abused the substance if he or she consumes more than society considers "normal"—usually more than two drinks a day for men and one for women. For people under the legal drinking age of 21, consuming any amount of alcohol is considered abuse. Using more prescription medication than a doctor orders or using any substance—such as glue—for purposes other than that for which it was intended is also considered abuse, as is any use of illegal drugs such as marijuana, cocaine, heroin, LSD, or methamphetamines.

ALCOHOL ABUSE

In 2004 the Centers for Disease Control and Prevention (CDC) released figures on the consequences of alcohol abuse in the United States. Each year about 75,000 people die as a result of consuming too much alcohol, approximately 35,000 from diseases such as cancer and cirrhosis of the liver and 40,000 from alcohol-related accidents, including automobile accidents. Men accounted for about three-quarters of the deaths from alcohol abuse in 2001; people under the age of 21 accounted for 6 percent of those who died as a result of alcohol abuse that year.

Fact Or Fiction?

Thanks to all the work done by Mothers Against Drunk Driving (MADD) and other such organizations, alcohol-related fatalities continue to decline.

Fact: Alcohol-related traffic fatalities declined from 60 percent of all traffic fatalities in 1982 to 42 percent in 1995, but have not declined further.

DID YOU KNOW?

Blood–Alcohol Levels and Behavior

Blood Alcohol Level	Predictable Behavioral Effects
Impaired (Use caution) 0.02–0.03%	Nontolerant drinkers begin to feel some effects such as mild relaxation and light-headedness.
0.04–0.05%	Most people feel relaxation and warmth; judgment is somewhat impaired.
0.06–0.07%	Euphoria or intensification of existing mood; deficits in motor coordination and reaction time; less ability to make rational decisions; driving is risky.
0.08–0.09%	Euphoria with increasing disorientation; clear impairment of motor skills; slurred speech; no recognition of mental and motor deficits; poor decision making; driving is dangerous.
Intoxicated (Needs close observation) 0.10–0.12%	Emotions are extremely exaggerated; lack of coordination and balance; thought and judgment are markedly impaired; recognition of impairment is lost; driving is extremely dangerous.
0.13–0.15%	Euphoric feelings have given way to dysphoric (unpleasant) feelings, difficulties in walking, talking, or standing; "blackouts" possible, loss of control over behavior; accidents.
Medical emergency (Seek medical care immediately) 0.25%	Dysphoric mood or numbness; all mental, physical, and sensory functions are severely impaired; nausea and vomiting; high risk of accidents; many people pass out.
0.30%	Little comprehension of environment; loss of consciousness likely; difficult to arouse.
0.35%	Loss of consciousness; physiology at the level of surgical anesthesia; death due to respiratory arrest is possible.
0.40%	Comatose; death due to respiratory arrest is likely.
0.45%	Deep coma and death due to anesthesia of nerve centers controlling respiration and heartbeat.

Source: What You Should Know about Alcohol and Drug Policy, Substance Abuse, and Health Risks, http://www.haverford.edu/healthservices/alcohol.pdf.

"We seem to be stalled or stuck at relatively the same fatality rate," said Dennis Utter, a statistician for the National Highway Traffic Safety Administration.

In May 2000 the *Journal of the American Medical Association* revealed that almost two-thirds of children under the age of 15 who died as a result of drunk driving between 1985 and 1996 were riding with a drunk driver, often a parent. This statistic shocked many people who had assumed that child passenger deaths due to drunk driving were most often caused when a drunk driver collided with a car carrying children. To make matters worse, only about 18 percent of those children were wearing seat belts at the time of the fatal crash; in fact, seat belt use decreased as the driver's blood alcohol content increased.

Underage drinking has been identified as a serious and growing problem in the United States. In 1997, the National Highway Traffic Administration reported that 21 percent of drivers between the ages of 15 and 20 who died in automobile crashes were driving drunk. Nearly half of all swimming and diving accidents involving young men were also alcohol-related, according to the U.S. surgeon general. In 2002, Richard Yoast, director of the American Medical Association's Office of Alcohol and Drug Abuse told an interviewer from CBS News that death was not the only danger posed by alcohol to young people. "Children who started drinking before the age of 15 had a much higher risk of having long-term lifelong alcohol problems and alcoholism than those who started after that," said Yoast. "The brain is still developing up until the early 20s. In fact, the adolescent brain is less resilient than the adult brain."

Binge drinking and alcohol poisoning occur with alarming regularity on American college campuses, despite efforts on the part of college administrators to educate students on the dangers of drinking too much too fast. Approximately 44 percent of college students have engaged in binge drinking, which is defined as having five or more drinks in a row for men and four or more in a row for women, according to the Harvard School of Public Health College Alcohol Study Surveys (1993–2001).

Alcohol poisoning can occur as a result of binge drinking and is frequently fatal. Because alcohol is a depressant, consuming too much in a short period of time can lead to death because it affects the part of the brain that controls breathing and heart rate. About 50 college students die of alcohol poisoning each year. In 2004 those victims included a young woman at Colorado State University who died after having 40 drinks at a fraternity party; a member of a fraternity at the University of Oklahoma whose blood-alcohol content was five times the legal limit; and a University of Arkansas student who died in an off-campus apartment after consuming a dozen beers and taking a painkiller and an antianxiety drug.

Q & A

Question: How can I tell if someone is the victim of alcohol poisoning and what can I do to help?

Answer: Signs to look for include vomiting, mental confusion, seizures, unconsciousness, difficulty awakening, and slow, shallow breathing. If you suspect alcohol poisoning, call 911 immediately. Do not leave the person alone and do not assume that he or she will "sleep it off." Turn the person so that he or she is lying on one side to keep the airway open in case of vomiting.

DRUG ABUSE

According to the 2001 National Household Survey on Drug Abuse (NHSDA), 15.9 million Americans 12 years of age and older used illegal drugs during the month prior to the survey. Of this number, 10.8 percent were between the ages of 12 and 17. According to the CDC, 19,698 people died in 2000 from drug use. This figure includes overdoses as well as other kinds of injury-related deaths that resulted from drug use.

Inhalants can be particularly dangerous. Inhalants are products that produce an intoxicating effect when breathed in through the nose or mouth. Many such products can be found around the house, including glues, solvents, lighter fluids, and some paint products. According to the 2001 NHSDA, more than 18 million people ages 12 and older reported using an inhalant at least once. Inhalants have been known to cause SSD (sudden sniffing death) syndrome. As oxygen is depleted from the body, any physical activity can cause sudden heart failure.

Beginning in 2001, many emergency rooms saw a rash of young people suffering from overdoses of over-the-counter cough and cold medicine. These overdoses were the result of what has been called "robotripping" or "dexing," deliberately overdosing on a medicine called dextromethorphan, which is found in certain brands of cold medicine. At least a half a dozen deaths have resulted from this practice.

So-called club drugs are also used by some young people. These drugs, which are associated with "raves" and dance clubs, include ecstasy, Rohypnol, ketamine, GHB, and LSD. Some of these drugs are colorless and tasteless and can be added to a person's drink without his or her knowledge. Between 1995 and 1998, about 2,700 deaths—mostly of young people—were associated with club drugs, according to the Drug Abuse Warning Network.

PREVENTING DRUG AND ALCOHOL ABUSE

Join Together, a project of Boston's University's School of Public Health, is designed to help communities prevent problems resulting from drug and alcohol abuse. As part of this effort, Join Together has issued a pamphlet entitled "10 Drug and Alcohol Polices That Will Save Lives." Three of the 10 policies deal specifically with preventing underage drinking. They are:

- Increase alcohol prices, through taxes, particularly on beer
- Limit alcohol advertising and promotional activities that target young people
- Adopt laws (such as graduated drivers' licenses) that will prevent alcohol-related deaths and injuries among young people

Four of the policies focus on treating drug addiction, including requiring insurance companies to pay for treatment programs, developing medications that effectively treat addiction, and screening for substance abuse by both primary-care and emergency-room doctors at every visit.

See also: Death, Unexpected and Planned; Dying, The Statistics of; Violent Death

FURTHER READING
Draper, S. *Tears of a Tiger.* New York: Pulse, 1996.
Keizer, G. *God of Beer.* New York: HarperCollins, 2002.

▉ DYING, THE PROCESS OF

Fewer than a hundred years ago, most Americans saw death as a natural part of life and most knew how to recognize when someone was dying because they had seen grandparents, parents, brothers and sisters die at home. As medical advances seemingly began to offer a cure for most illnesses, however, fewer and fewer people died at home, and Americans became strangers to death.

By the time Swiss doctor Elisabeth Kübler-Ross wrote her classic work *On Death and Dying* in 1969, most Americans had come to accept the idea that death was the province of doctors and that it was normal to die in the hospital hooked up to tubes and monitors. Kübler-Ross changed all that when she wrote about the process of dying as something natural and predictable; she reminded people that death with dignity was a basic right.

Partially as a result of Kübler-Ross's insights into the psychology of dying, the **hospice** movement began in the United States. The goal of hospice is to help people spend their final days in a peaceful environment, free of pain but alert enough to interact with family and say good-bye. With the assistance of hospice, many people can die at home in their own beds—or in a homelike hospice facility—without pain, breathing machines, or monitors. What this means for family members, however, is that they may need to be educated in what to expect as their relative dies and how they can help their loved one have a dignified and peaceful death.

THE PSYCHOLOGY OF DYING

Kübler-Ross made significant contributions to the understanding of the psychology of dying with her model of the stages of dying. She noted that people typically go through a series of psychological steps before they can accept the idea of their own death. These stages are denial ("This can't be happening," "I'm too young to die"); anger, bargaining ("Please, God, if only you'll let me live . . ."); depression; and finally acceptance. Not everyone goes through all the stages, according to Kübler-Ross, nor do people move through the stages smoothly and steadily.

Other researchers have proposed different models since Kübler-Ross proposed hers in 1969. They believe her model is too prescriptive, seeming to suggest that to die correctly, one must progress in a certain way. But it seems clear both that most people do eventually accept the reality of what is happening to them in the process of dying, and such acceptance paves the way for a more peaceful death because it allows the dying person to detach him or herself from life and prepare for death.

PHYSICAL CHANGES ASSOCIATED WITH DYING

According to the Hospice Foundation of America, a family can expect to see the following physical changes as a person approaches death:

- Sleepiness
- Confusion
- Vision changes
- Strange or inappropriate comments
- Repetitive or restless movements
- A decrease in activity and communication
- A decreased interest in eating and drinking
- A drop in body temperature, by a degree or more
- Falling blood pressure
- Cool hands and feet (because of diminished circulation)
- Changes in breathing. These include rapid breathing alternating with no breaths, known as "Cheyne-Stoking," after the person who first described the behavior, and gurgling or rattling sounds when breathing.
- Changes in skin color. Skin may become pale or even blue.
- Changes in the appearance of the fingernails. The beds of the nails may change from pink to a bluish color.
- Unresponsiveness
- Coma

There are many things families can do to help their relative through the process of dying. First and foremost, families should remember that hearing is the last of the senses to stop functioning. Even if the patient seems to be unresponsive, he or she may still be able to hear and might benefit from continued, comforting, affectionate talk. It is also important not to say things that might disturb the patient, even if he or she seems unable to hear.

If the patient is confused, family members should try to orient him or her. It is not a good idea to say things like "Do you know who I am?" Gently tell the patient who is in the room and who is talking: for example, "Hi, Dad. It's me, Tom. I'm here beside the bed."

To help with vision problems, family members should be sure that there is enough indirect light in the room and to sit near the bed so the patient can see them. Touch can also be important; holding the patient's hand may bring comfort.

The sound of rattling when the patient breathes may be disconcerting, but it is nothing to worry about. The noise is caused by secretions that build up in the throat and is not usually painful. It can sometimes help to raise the head of the bed to 30 or 45 degrees and turn the patient on his or her side. This may allow the patient to cough and relieve the buildup. Changing the patient's position every few hours can help protect against bedsores and may allow the patient to rest more comfortably.

One thing that may be difficult for families to understand and deal with is the patient's lack of interest in food and water. The Hospice Foundation of America states that in some cases giving food and water is considered an extraordinary means of prolonging life and can be discontinued. When the dying person reaches a certain point in the process, according to the Hospice Foundation, the lack of food and water is not painful; in fact, "there is a side effect . . . in which one's metabolism changes and the resulting elevated level of ketones produces a mild sense of euphoria." If a patient is not eating or drinking, families should not try to force food, but, instead, moisten the lips with water or offer crushed ice. Lip balm can be used to treat dry, chapped lips.

"Difficult Decisions: A Family Guide," published by the Columbia Brigham City Community Hospital, notes that many patients seem to hold off the final moment, waiting for "permission" to die from family members. Thus families can let the patient know that, when he or she is ready, it is all right to die. Sometimes patients seem to wait until family members leave the room, as if they want to spare family members the final moment.

Fact Or Fiction?

The process of dying is always painful.

Fact: In most cases dying itself is not painful at all. It is known that the body releases endorphins (brain chemicals that relieve pain) at death. If a person is dying of a disease that is painful, such as cancer, the pain can be managed through the use of such drugs as morphine. According to the Hospice Foundation of America, pain can be completely relieved in nearly all cases through the use of "multi-modality" approaches—that is, by combining drugs or other interventions.

BRAIN DEATH

Fifty years ago, the moment of death was easy for physicians to define. When the heart and lungs stopped working, an event referred to as **cardiopulmonary death,** the person was pronounced dead. However, since the development of mechanical **ventilators,** pacemakers, and other medical technologies that artificially prolong life, such a simple definition of death no longer works in every case. For example, today a person may be unable to breathe on his or her own, yet he or she can be kept alive almost indefinitely on a ventilator. The situation has been further complicated by advances in **organ transplantation,** which made it increasingly important to develop a definition of death that allows doctors to remove healthy organs for transplant without harming the donor. In 1968, Harvard Medical School issued a set of guidelines for "brain death," and in 1981, a presidential commission developed the Uniform Determination of Death Act (UDDA). This act recognizes brain death, which is defined as the "irreversible cessation of all functions of the brain," as a legal standard of death. In order for a patient to be pronounced brain dead, a physician must determine that:

- The patient cannot breathe without mechanical assistance;
- The pupils of the patient's eyes do not react to light; and
- The patient does not react to pain.

Bioethicists, people who study the ethical and moral issues of biological research, emphasize that doctors must go to great lengths to confirm brain death. Laws and policies differ from state to state and hospital to hospital, but in general, before someone can be declared brain dead there must be two examinations by two different doctors that confirm the complete absence of brain function. Many places require two **electroencephalograms (EEG)** 24 hours apart that show absence of electrical activity in the brain. If using EEGs to determine brain death, doctors must also ensure that the patient has not ingested certain drugs that can suppress brain activity. A scan that measures blood flow to the brain can be used instead of EEGs.

ORGAN DONATION

When a family member dies, the family may be asked to donate organs. For many, this is a difficult decision, especially if the patient has been declared **brain dead** but is being kept alive by artificial means. Families worry that the patient may suffer as the organs are removed or believe the patient may have a chance at survival if they waited. Thus, it is important for families to know that brain death is not the same thing as a **coma**. People in comas do, sometimes, recover. Brain death is, by definition, irreversible. The surgery to take transplantable organs does not hurt because people who are brain dead do not feel pain. Moreover, when organs are removed for transplantation, incisions are sutured and the body is not disfigured, so an open-casket funeral is still possible. There is never any cost to the family when organs are donated, and one person may be able to help as many as 50 other people in need of lifesaving procedures.

TEENS SPEAK

I Want to Be an Organ Donor

When I got my driver's license, I had to say whether or not I wanted to be an organ donor. The idea really grossed me out at first and I said "no." Some of my friends told me that if you were an organ donor and you were in an accident, the doctors wouldn't try as hard to save your life because they wanted your heart and stuff to transplant. But recently a guy at my school just had a kidney transplant, and if there hadn't been any kidneys available, he would have died. His name is Tim. Even though he's been sick a lot, he does everything. He's in a bunch of clubs and in all the plays and musicals. I can't imagine Tim dying, and I am so glad that someone was generous enough to donate organs so he could live. So I'm going to the driver's license bureau tomorrow to register as an organ donor.

It must be noted, however, that there are religious groups and doctors who question the very concept of brain death. For example, in a frequently cited article, "Brain Death–An Opposing Viewpoint," published in the *Journal of the American Medical Association* in 1979, Paul A. Byrne, with others, asserts, "The idea of brain death uniformly confound[s] [confuses] irreversible cessation of total brain function with the death of the human person. Much of the confusion comes from widespread misunderstanding of how the word 'death' is used and what it means. Cessation of total brain function, whether irreversible or not, is not necessarily linked to total destruction of the brain or to the death of the person."

A recent book, *The Definition of Death: Contemporary Controversies* (2000), is a collection of essays on all sides of the issue. It explores concerns about the adequacy of the definition of brain death, public policy issues around the world, questions regarding the difference between higher brain functions (thought, memory) and brain-stem functions (breathing), and whether the loss of higher brain functions only should be sufficient to declare someone brain dead. Other essays included deal with whether legal definitions of brain death have really helped to clarify the issue or merely confuse it.

NEAR-DEATH EXPERIENCES

In 1975, Raymond Moody, a psychologist and medical doctor, published *Life After Life*, in which he described what he called "near-death experiences." For the book, Moody interviewed a number of people who had died and been resuscitated. Many of them reported strikingly similar experiences: First they hear a buzzing noise and feel that they are traveling down a long, darkened tunnel. The patient can see his or her body from above and can see what is happening in the room. At some point, the patient meets other people and a "being of light," who replays the patient's life for him and helps him to see it in context. Then the patient reaches a stopping point and knows that he or she must return to life. The return is reluctant because the patient feels such love, joy, and peace in the "near-death" state. People who have had near-death experiences report that they are utterly changed by what happened to them and completely unafraid to die. Moody and others believe that near-death experiences confirm that there is an afterlife.

At first scientists did not take Moody seriously, but further research seemed to support the idea that these experiences were "real," at least in some sense. After the publication of Moody's book, many patients and their doctors revealed similar experiences, and in 1992, a Gallup poll found that as many as 13 million Americans had undergone a near-death experience. Further research, however, seems to demonstrate that it is instead the structure of the human brain itself that produces near-death experiences.

Karl L. R. Jansen, a British psychiatrist, in his article, "Using Ketamine to Induce the Near-Death Experience," in the 1996 *Yearbook for Ethnomedicine and the Study of Consciousness*, maintains that near-death experiences are caused by conditions such as low blood flow, low oxygen, or low blood sugar which, in turn, block the sites in the brain that receive nerve impulses. Jensen adds that near-death experiences can be induced by directly stimulating certain parts of the brain or through use of the drug ketamine. Ketamine was developed as a cat tranquilizer and was used extensively in Vietnam as an anesthetic, but its use for this purpose was stopped when soldiers complained of disturbing "out-of-body" experiences. Despite this kind of scientific research, however, many researchers and many people who have had near-death experiences themselves still believe that these experiences constitute proof that there is an afterlife.

Q & A

Question: Do people who are not dying ever have near-death experiences?

Answer: Yes. Certain hallucinogenic drugs and extreme fatigue can cause people to have out-of-body experiences that are very similar to the near-death experiences described by people who have died and been resuscitated.

AFTER DEATH

The human body continues to change after death. After a person dies, many of his or her organs are still technically alive. Brain cells survive death by about five minutes, the heart by about 15 minutes, and the kidneys for nearly a half hour. Skin cells live for 24 hours or more. After death, **algor mortis**, a steady decline in body temperature, occurs. The temperature of the body eventually matches the temperature of the surrounding air. From five to 10 hours after death, **rigor mortis** sets in, which is the stiffening of the limbs of a corpse, occurring because of chemical changes in the muscles. It lasts for about three days, then disappears. **Livor mortis**, which is a purplish discoloration on the underside of the body, begins at the moment of death as the blood, no longer circulating in the body, settles and pools. Immediately after the death, the process of decomposition begins, as enzymes and bacteria begin to consume the corpse. If a body is buried in a coffin, usually within a year only the skeleton will remain.

See also: Stages of Death, The

FURTHER READING
Nuland, Sherwin. *How We Die: Reflections on Life's Final Chapter.* New York: Vintage, 1995.

■ DYING, THE STATISTICS OF

The statistics of dying involve numerical data that assist in the study of various aspects of death. For example, a study of mortality statistics (death rates) reveals that Americans are living much longer today than at any time in history. Two sets of numbers are important to understanding the huge changes in life span that have occurred over time. One set of numbers relates to life expectancy at birth—the average number of years an individual is expected to live. The second set of numbers focuses on infant mortality—the number of babies born out of every thousand that die before the age of one.

LIFE EXPECTANCY AND INFANT MORTALITY RATES

Scholars estimate the average person born 2,000 years ago lived about 25 years. By contrast, in the United States in 2002, according to the Centers for Disease Control and Prevention (CDC), the average person can expect to live 77.4 years. The people who have the longest expected life span in the world today live in Andorra, a tiny country in southwestern Europe. On average, Andorrans live 83.5 years, according to the 2002 *CIA Factbook*. The people with the shortest life span live in Mozambique, a country in East Africa. On average, people there live 37.5 years.

Q & A

Question: How are statistics collected for the *National Vital Statistics Report*?

Answer: Researchers gather information from death certificates. A death certificate is a legal document that gives the date, location, and cause of a person's death. Usually the certificate is signed by a physician or the coroner, a public official whose job it is to determine the cause of death.

More than 2,000 years ago, 250 of every 1,000 infants died in their first year. In the United States in 2002, infant mortality was seven per 1,000. Sweden has the lowest infant mortality rate in the world, with 3.44 deaths per 1,000. The United States ranks 28th in the world, according to the 2002 *National Vital Statistics Report* (*NVSR*), due to disparities in prenatal and postnatal care available to rich and poor Americans. Angola, a West African nation, has the highest infant mortality rate in the world. On average, 191 of every 1,000 babies in Angola die before their first birthday.

Life-span statistics can also be examined from a variety of perspectives, including age, sex, race, and ethnicity. In the United States, for example, women tend to live longer than men, according to the *NVSR*. In 2002, a white woman's life expectancy in the United States was 80.3 years, while a white man could expect to live an average of 75.3 years. The expected life span for African Americans is significantly lower, 75.7 years for women and 68.9 for men. Infant mortality is also higher for African Americans, 14.3 per 1,000 births, as opposed to 5.9 per 1,000 births for whites.

CAUSES OF DEATH

Causes of death can vary greatly. Many researchers focus on particular age groups.

DID YOU KNOW?

Leading Causes of Death Among Children Ages 1–14, 2001

Source: National Center for Health Statistics.

Adults

In 2002, the *NVSR* identified the 15 leading causes of death among American adults. Heart disease led the list, followed by **malignant neoplasms**, or cancerous tumors. Third on the list were **cerebrovas-**

cular diseases, strokes and other diseases that affect the blood flow to the brain. Chronic lower respiratory diseases—including emphysema, chronic bronchitis, and cystic fibrosis—ranked fourth on the list, with accidents fifth. The other major causes of death, in descending order, are diabetes; influenza/pneumonia; Alzheimer's disease; nephritis/nephrosis (kidney diseases); septicemia (septic shock, or blood poisoning); suicide; chronic liver disease, including cirrhosis; hypertension (high blood pressure) and hypertensive kidney disease; pneumonitis (inflammation of the lungs caused by breathing in chemicals or dustlike particles of substances such as fungus); and homicide.

The placement of blood poisoning on this list may be surprising to those who assume that such infections are rare and easily curable. Not so. In fact, according to former surgeon general C. Everett Koop, about two-thirds of all cases of blood poisoning occur while a patient is hospitalized. Despite the efforts of hospitals to ensure a sterile environment, bacteria may be transmitted to patients by a variety of surgical or diagnostic procedures. Those with impaired immunity, particularly newborns and the elderly, are at greatest risk.

Infants

Twenty percent of infant deaths in the United States in 2002 were caused by congenital malformations, deformities, and chromosomal abnormalities. That is, as the fetus developed, something in the process went wrong, causing the child to be born with a condition that would not allow the newborn to survive.

The second-leading cause of infant mortality was short gestation—that is, the baby was premature and therefore born with a low birth weight. A short gestation can be caused by poor prenatal care and maternal drinking, smoking, or drug use. The third most frequent cause of infant mortality in 2002 was sudden infant death syndrome (SIDS), which is defined as the sudden death of an apparently healthy infant while sleeping. The causes of SIDS are unknown, although some researchers think that many of the victims have underdeveloped hearts and lungs. To prevent SIDS, parents are urged to not allow their babies to sleep face down and make sure they are not too warm while sleeping.

Teens

The major causes of death among teens in the United States differ from those of other Americans in that they have nothing to do with disease. The primary cause of death among young people ages 15–24 in 2002 was unintentional injuries, including automobile crash–related deaths. Although many factors contribute to fatal automobile crashes, inexperience is among the most significant, as is the fact that teens tend to drive smaller cars, which offer less protection in the event of a crash.

Teens also die from homicide at much higher rates than adults; it is the second-leading cause of death for this age group. Gang violence is responsible for as many as one-third of teen homicides.

The third most frequent cause of death among teenagers is suicide. About 1 percent of all teenagers attempt suicide and about one percent of those succeed, which means that about one in 10,000 teens dies each year from suicide; girls are more likely to attempt suicide than boys, but boys succeed four times more often. The cause of many suicide attempts is **depression**, a mental disorder characterized by feelings of sadness and despair. Substance abuse is also blamed for some teen suicides.

Statistics about death provide a variety of information to scientists and policy makers that can lead to prevention and treatment. In 2002, for example, the rate of death due to Alzheimer's disease for the entire population increased by 5.8 percent, while the rate of death due to cancerous tumors decreased by 3 percent. Such a change may help scientists and legislators determine how to allocate research dollars. While death cannot be prevented, studying the statistics about who dies, for what reasons, where, and under what circumstances can lead to longer, healthier lives.

See also: Teenage Deaths; Violent Death

FURTHER READING
Wendel, Helmut F., et al. *Vital Statistics of the United States 2004: Births, Life Expectancy, Deaths, and Selected Health Data (Vital Statistics of the United States).* Lanham, MD: Bernan Press, 2004.

■ ELDERLY MEN, AGING OF

Elderly is a difficult term to define. In a nation in which most people do not live past the age of 50, a 40-year-old might be considered elderly. On the other hand, a healthy 60-year-old man in the United

States might consider himself middle-age and define elderly, as one wit did, as "10 years older than me." As a general rule, however, an elderly person is usually defined at present as anyone over the age of 65, which is the age at which most people in the United States begin to retire.

As people age, they experience many changes in their bodies. They may find that aches and pains keep them from doing the things they once enjoyed, or they may discover that their eyesight or hearing is less acute. Some aspects of aging affect men and women alike. Other aspects of aging affect men and women differently; they are subject, in some cases, to different illnesses. They may also react differently to many life events.

DRIVING AND INDEPENDENCE

As men and women age, they often find it more difficult to drive a car. Changes in vision may reduce the ability to see to the side (peripheral vision) and impair depth perception. Hearing loss, if it causes people to pay substantially less attention to what is going on around them, can also make driving dangerous. Older people may also react more slowly to changes in traffic conditions, which can lead to car crashes.

People with Alzheimer's disease or other forms of **dementia**—diseases that affect the brain and diminish mental functioning—may even forget the rules of the road or panic because they do not know where they are. Some medications may cause dizziness or drowsiness. Because of these and other factors, drivers over the age of 65 have more crash deaths per mile than any group except teenaged drivers, according to the Centers for Disease Control and Prevention. In 2000, the Department of Transportation reported that while older people represent 9 percent of the population, they are responsible for 13 percent of all traffic deaths and 17 percent of all pedestrian deaths. Overall, statistics suggest, the older the driver, the greater the risk of accident.

Although aging has a similar effect on the driving capabilities of both men and women, they differ in their responses to the prospect of giving up or limiting driving. Because driving is often associated with independence, some people, especially men, are reluctant to admit that they may no longer be able to drive safely. Many men associate driving with manhood and regard surrendering their driving privileges as equivalent to a death sentence. Women tend to be more willing to stop or limit their driving. According to the National Highway Traffic Safety Administration, the reluctance of men to

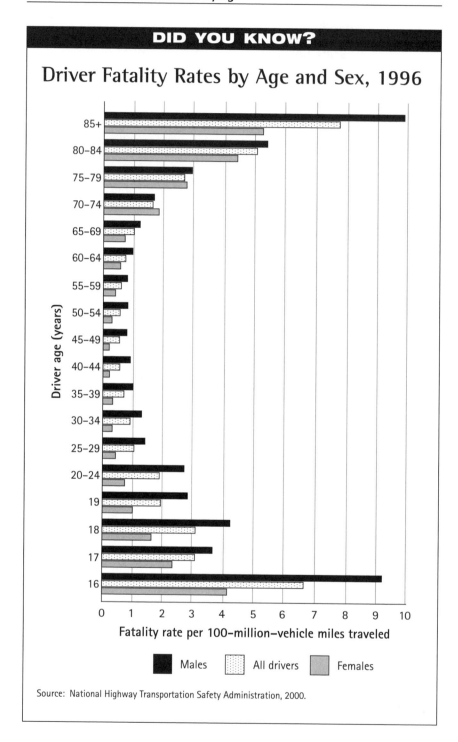

DID YOU KNOW?

Driver Fatality Rates by Age and Sex, 1996

Fatality rate per 100-million-vehicle miles traveled

Driver age (years)

■ Males   ▓ All drivers   ▓ Females

Source: National Highway Transportation Safety Administration, 2000.

give up driving may explain why twice as many men over the age of 85 die in automobile accidents than women.

DEPRESSION AND SUICIDE

According to the National Institute of Mental Health (NIMH) more than 2 million Americans over the age of 65 suffer from depression, and another 5 million may have subsyndromal depression, a form of depression that affects up to one in four seniors. Subsyndromal depression is characterized by depressive symptoms that affect well-being and quality of life but which do not meet the criteria for major depression. According to the NIMH, depression in the elderly may result from a variety of factors including illness, loneliness, and poverty. Researchers emphasize that depression is not a normal part of aging and can and should be treated.

An Australian study conducted by Kaarin Anstey and Mary Luszcz of the School of Psychology and Center for Aging Studies in Australia found that depression late in life occurs more often in women but has greater negative outcomes for men. They add that depression was more strongly associated with mortality for men but not for women.

According to the National Center for Injury Prevention and Control, 5,393 Americans over the age of 65 committed suicide in 2001. Of those, 85 percent were men. A NIMH study notes that white men over the age of 85 are five times more likely to commit suicide than any other portion of the population. Some people who try to kill themselves use less-than-lethal means, indicating that a suicide attempt may be a cry for help rather than a decision to end one's life. Not so with elderly men. Nearly three-fourths of the men over 65 who committed suicide used guns, which leave little room for error.

Yeates Conwell, a professor of psychiatry at the University of Rochester School of Medicine, points out that depression is largely undetected in the elderly. He has found that most seniors who committed suicide had visited a health-care provider within the previous month. Therefore, he urged primary-care physicians to pay attention to the possibility that depression may be hidden in a tangle of other medical problems.

FRACTURES

Elderly women are at significant risk for a condition called osteoporosis, which can cause bones to become brittle and break easily. Although osteoporosis is less common in elderly men, men with osteoporosis tend to be more at risk for death than women. According to a 1999 study that appeared in the medical journal *The Lancet,* broken bones were much more deadly for men than women. For example, 40 percent of men over 80 who broke their hips died within a year of the injury, whereas only about 30 percent of their female counterparts suffered the same outcome.

While women are aware that they are at risk for osteoporosis, men are not and therefore do not take steps to prevent or limit the progress of the disease. Men, like women, should have screenings to determine their bone density and use calcium supplements and weight training to strengthen their bones.

ANOREXIA

Most people think of **anorexia nervosa,** an eating disorder that leads to excessive weight loss, as a disease that primarily affects young women. However, researchers at the University of British Columbia in Canada found that the median age for death from anorexia nervosa was actually 69 for women and 80 for men. They also found that 21 percent of anorexia sufferers over the age of 45 were men, while only 10 percent of younger anorexia victims were men. Professors Paul Hewitt and Stan Coren, the researchers who conducted the study, do not know why older men are dying from anorexia but speculate that stress may be a factor. Yet another factor may be poor nutrition in general.

According to John Morley, director of geriatrics at St. Louis University School of Medicine, as many as 1 million men over the age of 80 may have nutritional deficits because they are unable to cook for themselves. Today many men know how to cook for themselves. However, many seniors grew up at time when cooking was thought of as women's work. As a result, many elderly men never learned even the basics of shopping for and preparing food. To address the problem, many social service agencies offer cooking courses for older men who have lost their wives or who are caring for ailing wives. Morley believes that learning to cook can help elderly men not only eat better but also socialize more, which is good for their health as well. He also values programs that provide the elderly with food, such as Meals on Wheels.

Young people can help elderly men face and overcome many of the problems they encounter as they age by staying connected and involved with elderly family members and neighbors. Offering to drive an elderly relative, visiting elderly neighbors, and staying alert to the possibility of depression or malnutrition are all simple things that teens can do to help elderly relatives and neighbors.

See also: Elderly Women, Aging of; Growing Old in America

FURTHER READING
Kosberg, Jordan I., and Lenard W. Kaye. *Elderly Men: Special Problems and Professional Challenges.* New York: Springer Publishing Co., 1997.

■ ELDERLY WOMEN, AGING OF

Elderly can be a subjective term. Places where average life expectancy is 50 years might define anyone above age 40 as elderly. In contrast, a healthy 60-year-old woman might consider herself middle-age in the United States. As a general rule, however, an elderly person is defined at present as anyone over the age of 65, which is the age at which most people in the United States begin to retire. Men and women age in similar ways but are affected differently by various physical problems and life events.

ALZHEIMER'S DISEASE

Alzheimer's Disease is a disorder that is marked by dementia—progressive mental deterioration, including memory loss, confusion, reduction of the ability to handle everyday tasks, and variations in alertness. It affects approximately 4.5 million Americans, according to the Alzheimer's Association.

People with Alzheimer's and other forms of dementia used to be referred to as **senile,** which is another word for "old." The term was often used in a negative sense. However, dementia is not a normal part of the aging process; all forms of the disease are illnesses.

While the causes of Alzheimer's are unknown, the symptoms seem to be affected by "plaques" and "tangles," structures that accumulate in the brain. Plaques are lumps of protein, and tangles are strands of a different protein that form inside cells. Scientists think that plaques and tangles may be responsible for the destruction of nerve cells. The loss of those cells may lead to the mental problems associated with Alzheimer's. However, scientists do not know why the plaques and

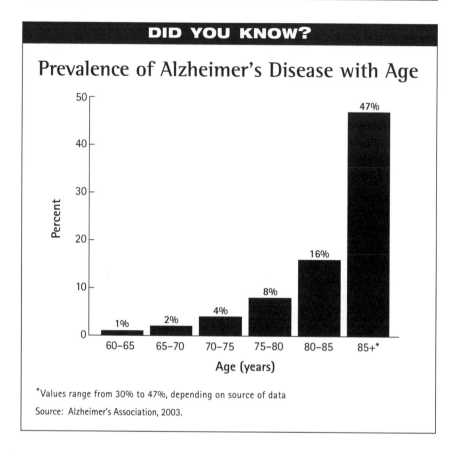

DID YOU KNOW?

Prevalence of Alzheimer's Disease with Age

*Values range from 30% to 47%, depending on source of data

Source: Alzheimer's Association, 2003.

tangles form, nor do they know whether these structures cause Alzheimer's or are a result of the disease.

The incidence of Alzheimer's disease increases with age. While one in 10 people over the age of 65 have Alzheimer's disease, almost half of those over 85 are afflicted. Alzheimer's is the fourth-leading cause of death among adults in the United States, and as the population ages, the number of those afflicted with the disease is likely to grow.

Although both men and women develop Alzheimer's, it has a disproportionate effect upon women. According to a 2001 article in the *American Journal of Epidemiology,* men and women do not differ in the rate or age at which they contract Alzheimer's; more women suffer from Alzheimer's disease, primarily because they live longer than men do. According to this study, the lifetime risk of contracting

Alzheimer's for women is nearly double that of men (32 percent for women and 18 percent for men).

Other studies, however, suggest that women may be more susceptible to Alzheimer's, even if one takes into account the fact that they live longer. An Italian study conducted by W. A. Rocca, S. Bonaiuto, and A. Lippi and published in the journal *Neurology* in 1990 suggested that women may be more likely than men to contract Alzheimer's because of hormonal or genetic factors.

Women also bear the burden of Alzheimer's disease in other ways as well. According to the Alzheimer's Association, more than 70 percent of Alzheimer's sufferers are cared for at home, and most of the caregivers are women. These caregivers are often elderly and under tremendous stress. The Alzheimer's Association notes that one-third of these family caregivers will die before the person they are caring for. Many caregivers work outside the home in addition to caring for their ailing relatives.

ARTHRITIS AND OSTEOPOROSIS

Arthritis and osteoporosis are diseases of the musculoskeletal system that disproportionately affect women. These diseases affect mobility and the ability to exercise and therefore have a negative impact on quality of life. Arthritis causes pain, swelling, and stiffness in the joints.

Osteoarthritis is the most common form of arthritis; it is caused by the breakdown of the cartilage that cushions the joints. As the cartilage is destroyed by age and injury, the bones rub together, causing pain. Rheumatoid arthritis is an **autoimmune** disease, a disease in which the body seems to attack itself. In rheumatoid arthritis, the body attacks the tissue surrounding the joints, causing the joints to become inflamed and painful. Although young people can be affected with rheumatoid arthritis, it is considered a disease of aging, since its incidence increases with age.

According to the Women's Health Alliance, women are three times more likely to suffer from osteoarthritis and rheumatoid arthritis than men. In fact, according to Somnath Pal, a professor at St. John's University College of Pharmacy and Allied Health Professions, "The most prevalent chronic disease affecting women is arthritis." He maintains that both forms of arthritis affect more than 600 of every 1,000 women past the age of 75.

Osteoporosis is a disease in which the bones weaken and break, sometimes without an external cause such as a fall. The bones most often affected by osteoporosis are those of the spine, hip, and wrist. Especially dangerous to elderly women are fractures of the spine and hip, which may impair mobility and even lead to death. According to the National Osteoporosis Foundation, osteoporosis affects 10 million people in the United States over the age of 50, and more than 80 percent of them are women.

BREAST CANCER

Although breast cancer can affect women of any age (and can actually affect a small percentage of men as well), one of the major risk factors associated with the disease is age. Women under the age of 40 have a relatively low risk of breast cancer, while women over the age of 70 have a significantly increased risk. According to the Susan G. Komen Breast Cancer Foundation, 77 percent of women diagnosed with breast cancer are over the age of 50. According to the National Breast Cancer Foundation, in 2004 alone, more than 43,000 women and 400 men died of breast cancer. The good news is that early detection is increasing survival rates. Today, if breast cancer is detected early, 95 percent of those diagnosed will survive for five years or more.

Some recent studies indicate, however, that older women do not receive aggressive treatments for breast cancer, leading to unnecessary mortality. For example, a study done by Jeanne S. Mandelblatt of Georgetown University Medical Center suggests that older women were much less likely to be offered radiation therapy as a treatment option than younger women.

AGEISM

Many elderly people in the United States are subjected to ageism. In a 2003 statement before the Senate Special Committee on Aging, Daniel Perry, executive director of the Alliance for Aging Research, defined ageism as "a deep and often unconscious prejudice against the old, an attitude that permeates American culture." While negative stereotypes of the elderly are directed at both men and women, women seem to suffer more from ageism than men.

According to Linda M. Woolf of Webster University, older women are often the butt of jokes and are regarded as unhealthy, dependent, and passive. In a 1982 study published in *Gerontologist*, F.H. Nuessel notes ageist vocabulary for women is more contemptuous because it represents them as "thoroughly repugnant and disgusting." Not surprisingly, many older women tend to view themselves negatively and go to great lengths to hide the effects of aging. Ageism not only affects their self-perception but also may influence their earning power and their ability to secure a desirable job.

POVERTY AND LONELINESS

Because women tend to live longer than men (by about five years) and tend to marry men who are older than they are, women are more likely to become widows than men are to be widowers. According to Andrew Scharlach and Esme Fuller-Thomson of the University of California at Berkeley, 12.8 percent of all women in America are widows, as are two-thirds of women over 75.

Q & A

Question: Since women live longer than men, about what percentage of the population over age 100 are women?

Answer: About 80 percent of U.S. **centenarians,** or people over 100 years old, are women. According to the U.S. Census Bureau in 2004, 76,000 centenarians resided in the United States, and some researchers believe that centenarians are the fastest-growing segment of the population.

Older women are also more likely to be poor than older men. According to the U.S. Census Bureau, 6.8 percent of the elderly poor are males, while 13.6 percent are females. Part of the reason that older women face poverty is that many stayed home to rear their children or worked in lower-paying jobs than men. Because women live longer than men, they also end up spending more on medical care and using up whatever pensions they have long before their death.

On the positive side, many elderly women survive the death of a spouse better than elderly men do. Women show greater resilience and ability to cope. Indeed, elderly women who have an adequate income after retirement report that their lives are full and satisfying.

See also: Elderly Men, Aging of; Growing Old in America

FURTHER READING
Gannon, Linda R. *Women and Aging: Transcending the Myths.* New York: Routledge, 1999.

■ GRIEVING, THE PROCESS OF

The intense sorrow people experience by the loss of a loved one is called grieving. Death is not the only loss people grieve. They may also grieve other losses.

WHAT IS GRIEF?

Many psychologists and sociologists who discuss grief make a distinction between grieving and **mourning**. While grief is an emotion that is personal and subjective, mourning is the public expression of grief–the behaviors that other people see. Thus, while a family may mourn together, following their cultural and religious rituals, they grieve individually, each in his or her own way. Many psychologists believe that ritualized mourning eases the grieving process.

TEENS SPEAK

I Hated the Whole Idea of a Funeral Before I Had to Go to the One for My Dad

When my dad died, I told my mom that I didn't want anything to do with the funeral stuff. Caskets, cemeteries, morticians, funeral homes—it all just grossed me out. But I could see that I really hurt Mom's feelings when I said that, so I went along with the whole thing for her sake. And, you know what, I was surprised to find that all the things I had dreaded—the wake, the viewing, the crying, the casket— they all actually helped me and my Mom to get through Dad's death. The religious parts were solemn and dignified and very comforting, and the visits and cards from people— and even the crying—really showed how many people loved my dad too. A lot of my friends feel like I did about funerals, so I've tried to share my experience with others— just in case they have to go through it.

As individual as grief is, it also has predictable patterns and outcomes. Experts on death and dying, notably Elisabeth Kübler-Ross,

John Bowlby, and George Engel, have outlined stages through which they believe a grieving person passes.

The best known of the "stage theories" of grief is Kübler-Ross's model. Kübler-Ross was a Swiss-born physician who wrote extensively about death and helped to found the **hospice** movement in the United States. Although she originally developed the stages to demonstrate what a dying person goes through, her model has also been applied to the grief process. The stages are:

- Denial. Many people go through a period during which they simply cannot accept that a loss has occurred. This stage may serve a psychological function in that it helps the person prepare for the eventual pain of loss.

- Anger. Anger is often accompanied by other emotions such as sadness and guilt once the reality of the death begins to sink in. People may become angry with the deceased for leaving, with themselves for things they may have done to hurt the deceased, or with others whose grieving style does not match their own.

- Bargaining. In this stage, the grieving person may try to bargain with himself or herself or with God to ask for a second chance. Even though the person knows the loss has occurred, he or she may still hope for a reprieve: "Please let it be a dream . . ."; "If only I had . . .".

- Depression. This is the stage most people think of when they consider grief. The individual feels sad and may cry often. He or she may withdraw from others and have trouble eating or sleeping. Some people need psychological counseling to move successfully through this stage.

- Acceptance. During the stage, the grieving person accepts the loss and begins to show interest in going on with life, even though he or she still feels the loss and remembers the loved one.

It is important to remember that many people do not progress through the stages in an orderly fashion and some may skip stages entirely. There is also no set timetable for moving through the stages.

John Bowlby, a British psychiatrist who studied children who suffered serious emotional damage from having lost those they loved, has identified four stages in the grieving process. Those stages are:

- Numbness or Protest. A stage similar to Kübler-Ross's idea of denial, in which the grieving person may be in shock and unable to acknowledge the loss.

- Disequilibrium. The word *disequilibrium* means "out of balance." During this stage, the grieving person thinks obsessively about the loss and may cry and feel anger and guilt.

- Disorganization and despair. The grieving person may not be able to carry on with normal activities. He or she may feel fearful, helpless, and may withdraw from social contact.

- Reorganization. This stage is similar to Kübler-Ross's idea of acceptance, in that the grieving person begins to think about living a normal life again.

George Engel was a psychiatrist who developed a **biopsychosocial** model of disease—meaning that disease may be caused by a combination of factors, including biological and emotional factors. Engel proposed five stages:

- Shock and disbelief. A stage similar to the first stages of both Kübler-Ross and Bowlby, in which, Engel notes, numbness is the primary way people seem to protect themselves against the pain of a loss.

- Developing awareness. As the grieving person becomes fully aware of the loss, he or she expresses a variety of feelings, including helplessness, anger, frustration, and despair.

- Restitution. During this stage, the grieving person performs the rituals he or she associates with death. Engel feels, as do many researchers, that these rituals help individuals accept the loss.

- Resolution of the loss. During this stage, the person processes the loss and is preoccupied with it for a period of time. During this stage, the grieving person usually begins to return to normal activities.

- Recovery. The grieving person accepts the loss and goes on with his or her life.

DID YOU KNOW?

Stages of the Normal Grief Response: A Comparison of Models by Elisabeth Kübler-Ross, John Bowlby, and George Engel

Kübler–Ross	Bowlby	Engel	Possible Duration	Likely Behaviors
I. Denial	I. Numbness/protest	I. Shock/disbelief	Occurs immediately upon experiencing the loss. Usually lasts no more than two weeks.	Individual refuses to acknowledge that the loss has occurred.
II. Anger	II. Disequilibrium	II. Developing awareness	In most cases, begins within hours of the loss. Peaks within two to four weeks.	Anger is directed toward self or others. Ambivalence and guilt may be felt toward the lost object.
III. Bargaining		III. Restitution		The individual fervently seeks alternatives to improve the current situation. Attends to various rituals associated with the culture in which the loss has occurred.
IV. Depression	III. Disorganization and despair	IV. Resolution of the loss	A year or more.	The actual work of grieving. Preoccupation with the lost object. Feelings of helplessness and loneliness occur in response to realization of the loss. Feelings associated with the loss are confronted.
V. Acceptance	IV. Reorganization	V. Recovery		Resolution is complete. The bereaved person experiences a reinvestment in new relationships and new goals.

Source: Townshend, Mary. *Psychiatric Mental Health Nursing.* 4th ed. 2002.

Some grief researchers reject all of the "stage theories of grief" as too simplistic and perhaps even harmful. According to Kathleen Gilbert, professor of applied science at Indiana University, "Stage models have come under increasing scrutiny . . . Although not intended by the vast majority of writers, they often are seen as prescriptive rather than descriptive; individuals who 'haven't gone through the stages' may come to feel that they are not grieving 'right.'"

J. William Worden, professor of psychology at the Rosemead School of Psychology, has proposed a task model of grief. He suggests that the grieving person must:

- Accept the reality of the loss. According to Worden, an acceptance of the reality of a loss takes time. Many people are intellectually aware of the finality of a loss long before they are able to emotionally accept their loss.

- Work through the pain of grief. Worden emphasizes that the pain of grief is both physical and emotional. He views the pain as a task that must be experienced, arguing that those who fail to work through the pain may never recover.

- Adjust to a changed environment. The grieving person must accept a world without the loved person, a task which Worden says "can challenge one's fundamental life values and philosophical beliefs."

- Emotionally relocate the deceased and move on with life. Worden is not suggesting that people "forget" the deceased. Rather, he would like them to find a special place in their heart or memory for the deceased even as they begin to form new attachments.

Gilbert notes that, as with stage models, task models have been criticized because they seem to suggest that "grief tasks can be resolved and grief can be left behind." She suggests that many people experience recurrent bouts of grief throughout their lives but are still able to go on with the necessary tasks of daily living and experience joy and pleasure.

HOW LONG DOES GRIEF LAST?

According to Engel, grief has been successfully resolved when the grieving person can "remember comfortably and realistically both the pleasures and disappointments" of what has been lost. How long it takes to reach that acceptance depends on the individual and the nature of the loss.

According to psychiatric nurse Mary C. Townshend in *Psychiatric/ Mental Health Nursing: Concepts of Care* (2003), "The acute phase of normal grieving usually lasts six to eight weeks" and the entire process can take a year or more. Certain factors can extend the grieving process. It may take a parent longer to grieve for the loss of a young child, for example, than for an adolescent to grieve for the loss of an elderly grandparent.

KINDS OF GRIEF

If a person is unable to work through the grieving process, his or her grief may be labeled **pathological**—that is, indicative of a mental or psychological condition. People whose grief is considered pathological may need professional counseling services in order to recover. Worden has identified four types of pathological grief, or what some researchers have called "complicated" grief:

- Exaggerated grief. A grief that may get worse over time rather than better. The grieving person may become clinically depressed or self-medicate with drugs or alcohol.

- Masked grief. Grief that a person is unable to feel or express. Some families insist that everyone "carry on" and "keep a stiff upper lip" despite the loss of a loved one. Such requirements may lead some to experience **psychosomatic illnesses**—illnesses with an emotional rather than a physical cause— or behavior problems.

- Chronic grief. Grief that does not allow one to get on with his or her life. Some individuals continue to grieve well beyond the time most people are able to resolve a loss.

- Delayed grief. The failure to experience grief at the time of the loss. When individuals whose grief is delayed eventually do experience the loss, their grief may be overwhelming.

Grief researchers have identified at least two other kinds of grief: anticipatory and disenfranchised. Anticipatory grief is what people experience when they anticipate the loss of a loved one, most often due to a terminal illness. While grieving after the event tends to diminish over time, anticipatory grief, according to Mary Townshend, "may increase in intensity as the expected loss becomes more imminent."

According to Townshend, anticipatory grief may cause problems for some people. If a person completes the process of grief before the actual loss, he or she may become "detached" from the dying relative, leaving him or her feeling lonely and isolated. On the other hand, anticipatory grief can help some people move through the grieving process that occurs after a loss more quickly.

Disenfranchised grief occurs when society does not perceive the grieving person as having a "right" to the emotions he or she is experiencing. According to Gilbert, disenfranchised grief may arise from a number of losses, including miscarriage, giving a newborn child up for adoption, the death of a pet, and the death of an ex-spouse or lover. People experiencing disenfranchised grief have the added burden of hiding their grief or subjecting themselves to criticism for "going overboard."

GRIEF AS A SPIRITUAL JOURNEY

Grief is not only a psychological or sociological experience but also a spiritual journey—one that can help people become stronger, more resilient, and more religious. Writer C. S. Lewis kept a journal as his wife, Joy, was dying of cancer (it was published as *A Grief Observed* in 1961). In the journal, he tracked the spiritual growth that he experienced through the grieving process. "Nothing" he writes, "will shake a man—or at any rate a man like me—out of his merely verbal thinking and his merely notional beliefs. He has to be knocked silly before he comes to his senses. Only torture will bring out the truth." Lewis, perhaps better than most, expresses what healing feels like, in all its beauty and power:

> It came this morning early. For various reasons, not in themselves mysterious, my heart was lighter than it had been for many weeks. For one thing, I suppose I am recovering physically from a good deal of mere exhaustion. And I'd had a very tiring but very healthy twelve hours the day before, and a sounder sleep; and after ten days of low-hung gray skies and motionless warm dampness, the sun was shining and there was a light breeze. And suddenly at the very moment when, so far, I mourned [Joy] least, I remembered her best. Indeed it was something (almost) better than memory; an instantaneous, unanswerable impres-

sion. To say it was like a meeting would be going too far. Yet there was that in it which tempts one to use the words. It was as if the lifting of the sorrow removed a barrier.

See also: Death and the Family; Loss of a Pet; Stages of Death, The

FURTHER READING
Rando, Therese A. *How to Go on Living When Someone You Love Dies.* New York: Bantam, 1991.

■ GROWING OLD IN AMERICA

It is commonplace to describe the United States as a youth-oriented society, one that worships the young and denigrates the old. The contrast is often made between American society and that of China, where older people are revered for their wisdom and experience.

One indicator of Americans' fear of aging is the increasing popularity of cosmetic surgery. In the 1980s, approximately 60,000 cosmetic procedures were performed each year; according to the Millennium Research Group, more than 8 million such procedures were performed in 2003.

What it means to grow old in America and what it *ought* to mean is becoming a pressing question as the population as a whole ages, thanks both to the number of baby boomers entering their sixth decade and to medical advances that allow people to live longer. The number of Americans who are over the age of 55 will nearly double by the year 2030, from 60 million (21 percent of the population) to 107.6 million (31 percent). Thus it becomes increasingly important to understand both the popular myths about aging and the reality of what it is like for most people to grow old.

AGEISM

Ageism is a term that was coined in 1969 by Robert Butler, who was the first Director of the National Institute on Aging. According to A.J. Traxler, professor of psychology and director of the Gerontology Program at Southern Illinois University, ageism is "any attitude, action, or institutional structure which subordinates a person or group because of age or any assignment of roles in society purely on the basis of age." Many studies have demonstrated that there is a strong tendency in America to devalue old people. For example, Webster

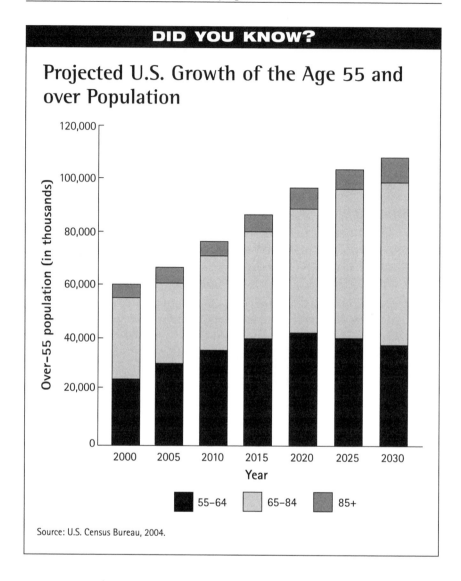

DID YOU KNOW?

Projected U.S. Growth of the Age 55 and over Population

55–64   65–84   85+

Source: U.S. Census Bureau, 2004.

University psychology professor Linda M. Woolf, in "Ageism: An Introduction," cites a number of studies that have looked at the portrayal of the elderly on television. She holds that research demonstrates that "the proportion of older individuals on television is underrepresented and when present, their image is primarily negative." She also notes that many jokes are based on very negative stereotypes of aging and tend to promote images of the elderly as forgetful, well past their sexual prime, and physically falling apart. There is even an entire subcategory of birthday cards designed to make fun of old age.

Negative stereotypes about old age, it turns out, start young. A study conducted by University of Alberta psychology professor Sheree Kwong in 2003, "An Early Start to Age Stereotyping: Children's Beliefs About an Older Experimenter," concluded that children as young as five already have negative stereotypes of older people. Professor Woolf agrees, citing a number of studies conducted over a 20-year period that "demonstrate that children and young adults often maintain a stereotypic and negative view of aging and older adults."

Ageism appears to have a number of extraordinarily negative consequences for older adults. First of all, many employers may believe that older workers are not as productive as younger ones, leading to the possibility of employment discrimination. Even though it is illegal in the United States to discriminate on the basis of age, the **American Association of Retired Persons (AARP)** reports that in 2002, nearly 20,000 age discrimination complaints were filed with the government's Equal Employment Opportunity Commission, the largest number ever. The long-term financial consequences of age discrimination in the workplace are potentially devastating to many older Americans.

Ageism also affects the quality of health care available to the elderly. The Alliance for Aging Research, in "How Healthcare Fails the Elderly," concludes that there are five important ways in which U.S. health care fails older people:

- People in the health professions do not receive adequate training in **geriatrics,** the medical specialty of caring for the elderly.

- Older patients do not receive the level of preventive care that younger patients do.

- Older patients are not screened for diseases and other health problems as often as younger patients.

- Older patients are usually not allowed to participate in drug trials, even though they are most likely to be the users of those drugs.

- Proven therapies that could help older patients are often ignored.

According to this report, the root of inadequate health care for American seniors lies in the tendency of both medical professionals and patients to view serious medical conditions as part of the process of growing old. As a result, health care providers miss millions of preventive and treatment opportunities each year, thus failing to enhance the lives of many older Americans.

In fact, disease is not a necessary or inevitable part of aging. The Baltimore Longitudinal Study of Aging, published by the National Institutes of Heath, urges medical professionals and patients to distinguish between the true effects of aging and those processes, including disease, that may appear or become more pronounced with time but are biologically irrelevant to the underlying mechanism of human aging. The study goes on to point out that while the incidence of disease increases with age, aging and disease are not synonymous. Aging is a normal consequence of the passage of time that takes place in everyone. Disease occurs in only part of the population.

Q & A

Question: What are some things doctors should be doing in order to provide better overall medical care for the elderly?

Answer: One of the most obvious is to check hearing. According to the *Journal of the American Medical Association*, nearly 40 percent of people over 65 have some hearing impairment. Most elderly Americans are not checked for hearing loss even though there are many treatments available that can correct hearing problems in most people. Pneumonia and influenza vaccines are other important preventative health measures that doctors can provide.

Perhaps the most devastating consequence of ageism is that these stereotyped negative ideas about old age can actually shorten life. Ageism is different from other kinds of stereotyping in that it is eventually internalized; that is, everyone—if they do not die young—will eventually be old, and all the negative ideas they ever had about aging may be turned on themselves, with potentially fatal consequences. A 2002 study published in the *Journal of Personality and Social Psychology,* "Longevity Increased by Positive Self-Perceptions of Aging," found that people who had positive ideas about what growing old would be like actually lived 7.5 years longer than those who had negative ideas, even when the researchers took into account such factors as age, gender, socioeconomic status, loneliness, and functional health. Because the results of this study were so significant, the authors call for a comprehensive remedy to the problem of "societally sanctioned denigration of the aged."

Another study published in 2004 by researchers at the University of Texas Medical Branch found that older people who had positive views of aging were significantly less likely to become frail. A 2004 study at North Carolina State University found that older adults exposed to negative stereotypes did poorer on memory tests than those exposed to positive stereotypes. Thus, the so-called memory loss sometimes experienced by older adults—often referred to jokingly as "senior moments"—may be caused less by age than by the fear of aging. In China, where the elderly are held in higher esteem, elderly subjects did nearly as well on tests of memory as younger subjects, according to a study by psychologists Rebecca Levy and Ellen Langer.

Fact Or Fiction?

Old people, like old dogs, can't learn new tricks.

Fact: Although older people may take a little longer to learn something new, most people are capable of learning throughout their life span. In fact, the very act of learning helps to keep the mind alert and active, according to Lawrence C. Katz, a professor of neurobiology at Duke University.

CONQUERING AGEISM

Jere Daniel, in a 1994 *Psychology Today* article, "Learning to Love Growing Old," reveals that a revolution in attitudes about age is in process and may well change the way society looks at and deals with growing old. Many theorists believe that ageism in the West stems from a fear of death. Because Westerners associate old age with death, they develop negative stereotypes about age in order to allow themselves to feel different from old people and hence distant from death. Many Eastern cultures, as well as many traditional societies, tend to see death as a normal and natural part of the life cycle. Perhaps as a result of these beliefs, they tend to respect and honor the elderly and the contributions they can make to society. According to Stephan Rechtschaffen, M.D., founder of the Omega Institute, "In our denial of death and the aging of the body, we have rejected the wisdom of the aged, and in doing so have robbed old age of its meaning and youth of its direction." A number of medical and social commentators, including Rechtschaffen, Sherwin Nuland (retired cardiologist and author of the 1994 book *How We Die*), and Betty Friedan (author of the 1963 book *The Feminine Mystique*, and considered by many to be the founder of the woman's movement) are actively involved in trying to change Americans' perception of old age. Rechtschaffen advocates what he calls "conscious aging," an awareness that our lives will end and that the final years are special and deserve to be savored and appreciated. In particular, both the elderly and the young must learn to appreciate the value of wisdom that comes with age. In an article, Jere Daniel notes that wisdom accumulates with time—but only among those who remain open to new experiences. It is the elderly themselves who must believe in their own worth and wisdom in order to change society's negative view.

IMAGES OF AGING IN AMERICA

There is some evidence that as the baby boomer generation approaches old age, perceptions of aging are shifting as well—in a more positive direction. The AARP recently released a summary of a 2004 telephone survey that was designed to measure the attitudes of Americans toward aging and the elderly. The survey included a list of 25 statements designed to measure how much knowledge people have about aging. Those who responded to the survey were "fairly knowledgeable" about aging. They understood, for example, that "older persons can learn" and that most of the elderly "can work or want work to do" and that most elderly people "feel healthy." Nevertheless, there were still many misconceptions. People who responded to the survey believed that most elderly persons live below the poverty line. (Actually, according to the U.S. Census Bureau in 2000, only about 10 percent of elderly fit that description.) They also believed many elderly people live in nursing homes (only about 4 percent do) and that the elderly cannot adapt to change. Overall, the survey noted, the less knowledge people had about aging, the more anxiety they had about growing older themselves.

A 2000 poll by the *Los Angeles Times* concludes that "old age is not a frightening prospect for most people; it does not signify a loss of independence [or] a drop in overall life satisfaction." When people over 60 were asked if they thought life would get better or worse as time went on, most said life would be better or about the same. Most of those over 60 who responded to the survey said they felt younger than their years and looked at least 15 years younger than their real age. Most of the people who responded to the survey said that they were not lonely and that they kept in close touch with family members; 85 percent of women and 76 percent of men said they see or speak with their children at least once a week. Most of the comments from the over-60 group about retirement were positive. However, 20 percent of the respondents said they sometimes worried about finances.

GROWING OLD GRACEFULLY

According to "How to Grow Old Gracefully," a publication of the University of California at Irvine Academic Geriatric Resource Center, there are five major things one can do in order to age well. They are:

- Keep occupied. Do not suddenly stop working at retirement. Develop new interests, volunteer, consult, start a new career.

- Make new friends. A support network is crucial in preventing depression. It is a good idea to have friends from all age groups.

- Give life a chance. Stay open-minded, try new things, take risks.

- Get into the spirit. Do not ignore the spiritual side of life. Whether through participation in organized religion or meditation, keep the spirit vigorous.

- Try to see the big picture. Coming to terms with age and looking back over their lives leads many elderly people to see this part of their lives as the best part.

Nutrition, exercise, and regular medical checkups are also crucial to a productive and happy old age.

TEENS SPEAK

What Old Age Looks Like

My great-grandmother just died at 93. She was the most amazing person I have ever known, and I hope I can be just like her when I am old. She had a career outside the home when she was young, working as a graphic designer while raising four sons. Then, when she retired from that, she became a Montessori teacher—at the age of 65. She taught little kids, four- and five-year-olds, until she was in her eighties, when she "retired" again.

Great-gran volunteered, traveled, and worked out several times a week in the same place as the members of the local professional hockey team, who really got a kick out of her. Her memory was sharp to the end. With some help from my dad and my uncles, she lived in her own home until the day she died. That's my idea of old age.

See also: Elderly Men, Aging of; Elderly Women, Aging of; Living Longer, Living Better?

FURTHER READING
Cohen, Gene D. *The Creative Age: Awakening.* New York: Perennial Currents, 2001.
Friedan, Betty. *Fountain of Age.* New York: Simon & Schuster, 1994.
Vaillant, George E. *Aging Well: Surprising Guideposts to a Happier Life from the Landmark Harvard Study of Adult Development.* New York: Little, Brown, 2003.

■ HELP AND SUPPORT

There are many varieties of assistance that are available to those who are dying and to their families and friends as they deal with the process of dying and the grief that follows death. Facing one's own death and dealing with the death of a loved one are two of the most difficult of life's experiences, and most people need a good deal of help and support to get through the process in a positive manner. In many cases people get the help and support they need from family and friends. If a family member is cared for at home, the work of caregiving may be shared by all family members. Neighbors may volunteer to sit with the person who is ill so caregivers can take time off. Friends may offer to cook meals or run errands.

After death, friends and neighbors often come together to mourn and to help to find ways to memorialize the person who has died through donations to charity and speeches of praise, called **eulogies**. It is customary for neighbors to bring food to the home of the person who has died to help the family. Perhaps the most appreciated and needed form of support after a death is the simple gift of listening to those who mourn the loss of someone they loved.

While many deal well with death without professional help, a considerable number of people do not. The good news is that, in addition to family and friends, there are many sources of help and support available to the dying and those they love.

HOSPICE

In 2004, the *Journal of the American Medical Association (JAMA)* published a study entitled "Family Perspectives on End-of-Life Care at the Last Place of Care," which concludes that many people dying in institutions have unmet needs —relieving symptoms, communicating with physicians, receiving emotional support, and being treated with respect. According to the *JAMA* study, most Americans (67.1 percent) die in hospitals and nursing homes, where they may not receive adequate end-of-life care. The study found that almost 25 percent of those who died in nursing homes did not receive appropriate treatment for breathing distress, and approximately 33 percent did not receive adequate pain medication. The families of those who died in hospitals reported similar difficulties. The study concludes, however, that family members with loved ones who received care at home with hospice services were more likely to report a favorable dying experience.

Hospice care may be delivered at the dying person's home or in a hospice facility. The primary goal of hospice is to provide **palliative care** to those who are dying. The word *palliative* refers to reducing the intensity of something; in the context of hospice, palliative care refers to providing both pain medication and emotional support in order to reduce the physical and emotional distress of dying. Hospice also provides services for family members to help them understand and cope with what is happening to their relative. Hospice also provides care

DID YOU KNOW?

National Hospice Usage by Client Age, Gender, Race, and Marital Status

Characteristic	Percent Distribution
Age	
< 45 years	3.9
45–54 years	5.0
55–64 years	11.5
65+ years	79.6
65–69 years	10.1
70–74 years	14.5
75–79 years	12.5
80–84 years	15.9
85+ years	26.5
Gender	
Male	49.8
Female	50.2
Race	
White	84.1
Black	8.1
Other or unknown	7.8
Marital Status	
Married	47.2
Widowed	33.2
Divorced or separated	5.7
Never married	7.7
Unknown	6.2

Source: Centers for Disease Control and Prevention, 2002.

for the family after their loved one dies, in the form of education and counseling. What hospice does not do, however, may be as important as what it does. Hospice care acknowledges that the patient is dying and thus does not provide treatment for the illness itself. Thus, the patient is spared invasive and sometimes painful procedures that may only prolong death.

According to a 2001 article in the *Journal of Computer Mediated Communications*, hospice care can even be delivered by videophone in areas where services may not be locally available. The authors note that fewer than 75 percent of those who need hospice care do not have access to it. Those living in rural areas and minority communities may be particularly underserved. This article reports preliminary results of a two-year study of what has been dubbed "telehospice" (TH) on patients in Michigan and Kansas. The study concludes that TH will not replace the need for traditional hospice visits, "but TH allows patients and caregivers to communicate quickly with members of the hospice care team."

FAMILY ACTIVITIES

Sometimes family members are at a loss as to how they can help the person who is dying. Most psychologists and grief therapists say that the single most important thing family members can do is simply to "be there." Holding hands, touching, and listening are invaluable gifts. If the dying person is able, however, there are many activities families can do together to ease the emotional pain of dying for themselves and the family member who is ill. Materials developed to accompany the PBS series on dying, *On Our Own Terms*, by Ann Villet-Lagomarsino suggest six such activities:

- Write a journal. Family members can recall and write down stories that help them remember happier times and the character and accomplishments of the relative who is dying.

- Collect and organize photos. Going through family photos with the person who is dying can provide hours of reminiscence. Placing loose photos in albums and adding captions provides time for recapturing memories—and results in a lasting document for the family.

- Plant a memory garden. If the dying person is able, work together to plant a tree or perennial garden that will serve as a remembrance of the person in years to come.

- Get a pet. The antics of a puppy or kitten can bring laughter and comfort. The pet will then become a reminder of the person who has died. (It is a good idea to get a doctor's approval for this, as some patients may be too ill or may have allergic reactions.)

- Get out of the house. If the dying person is able, traveling can help people keep up their spirits.

TEENS SPEAK

When My Friend Suzanne Was Dying, We Made a Scrapbook

I first met Suzanne in kindergarten—and we've been best friends ever since. I guess I should say we *were* best friends—because Suzanne died of leukemia last year. She was sick for almost a year before she died, and we knew for sure six months before that she wouldn't make it. I didn't know what to do or how to help except just to be around whenever I could. But my mom, who is into scrapbooking, came up with this terrific idea to make a scrapbook of Suzanne's life. I collected pictures and souvenirs from everyone at school and Suzanne's relatives, and I showed up one day with this huge box and tons of my mom's scrapbooking stuff—stickers, pens, colored paper. Suzanne and I spent hours and hours together putting this book together. We laughed a lot and we cried a lot—but I think we laughed more than we cried, which was great. When Suzanne died, her mother told me the scrapbook brought her more comfort than anything else, which made me feel a lot better too.

ART AND MUSIC THERAPY

Art and music therapy are used in a variety of situations to help people better understand their own feelings and emotions. People who practice these therapies are usually trained in either the visual arts or music as well as psychology. They encourage patients to draw or listen to music, and then help them interpret their reactions to what they've drawn or heard.

Both art and music therapy can be very effective in helping the dying come to terms with death. Paola Luzzatto, an art therapist at Memorial Sloan-Kettering Cancer Center in New York, uses art therapy to help patients express feelings or thoughts that they might find difficult to express in words. Lucanne Mcgill, program manager of music therapy at Sloan-Kettering, notes that music therapy can be particularly useful at the end of life, when communications may break down and a sense of isolation set in for the dying person. Since music is usually interpreted as a safe vehicle for expressions of sorrow, gentle tones, harmonies and melodies can refocus attention, soothe pain, ease struggle, and alter moods. Both art and music therapy can be done by the patient without a trained therapist and can also be done as part of a family activity.

SUPPORT FOR GRIEVING

After a loss, many people turn to professional grief counselors for help in coming to grips with what has happened to them. Particularly if the death has been a violent one, people may benefit from attending support groups where they can discuss their loss with others who suffered similarly. In addition to the kinds of support that are available locally, the Internet can serve as a tremendous resource for those who are grieving the death of a loved one.

In keeping with its mission to help survivors as well as the dying, the Web site for the Hospice Foundation of America provides an extensive list of organizations that offer specialized support to the dying and their survivors. For example, the Air Crash Support Network (ACSN) offers help to people who have been affected by an airplane disaster. In Loving Memory is a support group for parents who have lost an only child or all their children. The International Association of Firefighters (IAFF) provides assistance to the families of firefighters and paramedics. Rosetta Life helps those who are dying to document their lives in whatever artistic form they choose. The Dougy Center works with children and adolescents who have suffered a loss. The Tragedy Assistance Program for Survivors (TAPS) offers support to those who have lost a loved one in the armed services. Widow Net works with widows and widowers. The SIDS Alliance works with families who have lost a child to sudden infant death syndrome. The National Organization of Parents of Murdered Children offers support to parents whose children were victims of homicide. All of these organizations—and many, many others—have a presence on the Internet and can be easily found by searching for keywords or by the name of the organization. Many of these groups supply online support and discussion groups for those who are grieving, as well as links to local counselors and support groups.

Death is never easy, but no one has to deal with death alone and without support, as long as they are aware of what is available. The Hospice Foundation, the Association for Death Education and Counseling, the American Psychological Association, and many other such groups are working hard to get the word out and to educate the public about how to handle this very difficult life event.

See also: Dying, The Process of; Grieving, The Process of; Managing Death

FURTHER READING

Lehmann, Linda, et al. *Teens Together Grief Support Group Curriculum: Adolescence Edition: Grades 7-12.* New York: Brunner-Routledge, 2000.

Smith, Harold Ivan. *Death and Grief: Healing Through Group Support.* Minneapolis, MN: Augsburg Fortress Publishers, 1997.

■ LIVING LONGER: LIVING BETTER?

Since the 1960s, gerontologists, scientists who study the process and problems of aging, have developed a variety of templates or models that attempt to specify what "successful aging" should look like. In 1961, a "disengagement" model of old age was proposed by gerontologists Elaine Cumming and W. E. Henry. This model suggested that a successful elderly person was one who happily retired from work on schedule and proceeded to disengage from the world, until he or she did little but sit on a rocking chair waiting for death to come.

Such progressive disengagement, it was theorized, helped society cope with the death of the elderly, since by the time they died they were not particularly involved and would not, therefore, be particularly missed. According to Lucille B. Bearon, aging specialist at North Carolina University's Department of Family and Consumer Sciences and author of the 1996 study "Successful Aging: What Does the

'Good Life' Look Like?" "to social scientists of the 1960s, what was typical or common among older people may have shaped the perception of what was optimal or possible."

Since the 1960s, a number of other models of successful aging have been formulated. The 1970s saw the formulation of the "activity theory" (advanced by B. W. Lemon, V. L. Bengtson, and J. A. Peterson). This model proposed an active life as the most desirable one for the elderly. Bearon notes that this theory explains the surge of volunteerism and senior activism in the 1960s and 1970s. It may even have been responsible in part for public policies which underwrote the development of senior centers and other recreational facilities. Also in the 1970s, Robert Atchley proposed a continuity theory, suggesting that a successful old age was achieved if an elderly person could continue doing many of the same things in later life as he or she had done in middle age.

New models of successful aging were advanced in the 1990s, which regard the extent to which a person can continue to grow mentally and spiritually as the key to growing old successfully. One such theory, advanced by the Omega Institute for Holistic Studies, has been dubbed "conscious aging." This theory, according to Bearon, stresses the inner dimensions of experience and the key role of internal motivation as the foundation for action and the source of resilience for individuals as they age. Stephan Rechtschaffen, M.D., founder of the Omega Institute, believes that it is important for American society to learn to revere the wisdom of the elderly and that it is equally important for the elderly to appreciate what they have to offer the young.

In a 1991 article, "Aging Well: What Are the Odds?," C. D. Austin focuses on those members of the community who are not able to achieve a successful old age because of poverty, disability, or other factors. Many elderly poor have no health insurance and insufficient financial resources to purchase health care and, thus, do not benefit from many of the medical advances that help keep people healthy as they age. Those who suffer from disabling dementias such as Alzheimer's disease do not fit into models of successful aging. Clearly, for the American population as a whole to age successfully, issues such as racism and poverty must be addressed, and cures for illnesses that affect the mind must be sought.

Unquestionably, most of America's **baby boomers** who are moving from middle into old age over the next 20 years would reject any model of aging that confined them to rocking chairs. Most seem to envision an old age that incorporates many aspects of the gerontologists' later models. Bearon concludes her article by suggesting that the only really relevant measures of successful aging are in the eye of the beholder—that is, each individual must decide for himself or herself what the end of a good life looks like. Yet there seems little doubt that most Americans today would regard physical health, mental sharpness, and social connectedness as crucial to successful aging.

PHYSICAL HEALTH

According to the Centers for Disease Control and Prevention (CDC) in a 2004 report, "Healthy Aging: Preventing Disease and Improving Quality of Life Among Older Americans," the U.S. population has aged dramatically over the past 100 years and will continue to age at a very rapid rate. As the report points out, 100 years ago, only 3 million people in the United States were over the age of 65. Today, more than 33 million Americans fall into this age group, and that number is expected to double over the next 30 years as baby boomers age. This aging of America will trigger a huge demand for health care and social services.

Although some people associate disease with old age, there really is no inescapable connection. It is possible to grow old and die without ever suffering from conditions such as cancer, heart disease, or diabetes. In fact, most of the diseases that affect the elderly are "lifestyle" diseases and can be prevented through improved nutrition and exercise. Thus the prediction that the aging of America will result in soaring health-care costs may not be accurate—if people eat better and exercise more.

Thus, according to the CDC, research has shown that healthy lifestyles are more influential than genetic factors in helping older people avoid the deterioration that people traditionally associate with aging. People who are physically active, eat a healthy diet, do not use tobacco, and practice other healthy behaviors reduce their risk of chronic diseases. They also have half the rate of disability of those who do not.

Eating a healthy diet can be a real challenge for some among the elderly. Problems with teeth, gums, and digestion may interfere with what some people can eat. The senses of taste and smell diminish with age, causing some people to lose interest in eating. Loneliness and boredom

DID YOU KNOW?

The Dramatic Aging of America, 1900–2030

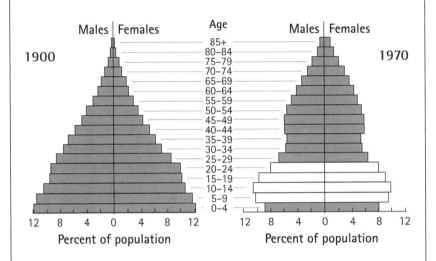

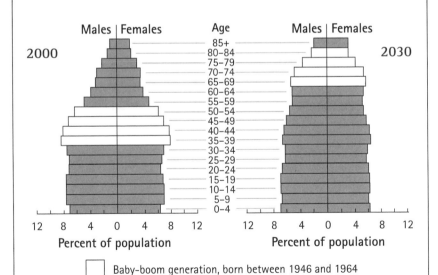

Baby-boom generation, born between 1946 and 1964

Source: U.S. Census Bureau, 2002.

may also contribute to an unhealthy diet, especially if individuals are too depressed to cook and rely on prepackaged meals or fast-food. According to a 2001 publication, "Staying Sharp: Current Advances in Brain Research," from the **American Association of Retired Persons (AARP)**, there are several keys to eating well as one ages:

- Eat plenty of whole grains, fruits, and vegetables.
- Drink water, at least five glasses a day, along with three glasses of other fluids.
- Reduce saturated fat intake.
- Reduce intake of trans-fatty acids, often listed on food labels as "hydrogenated vegetable oils."
- Choose healthy snacks.
- Take advantage of community food programs, such as Meals on Wheels, if necessary.

Exercise is a "key ingredient to healthy aging," says Professor David C. Nieman, of the Department of Health, Leisure, and Exercise Science at Appalachian State University. Nieman adds that of all age groups, elderly people have the most to gain by being active. Physician Joseph A. Buckwalter, in "Decreased Mobility in the Elderly: The Exercise Antidote," published in *The Physician and Sportsmedicine*, adds that it is never too early and rarely too late to launch a regular exercise program to prevent or reverse age-related decreases in mobility.

Some elderly people are caught in a vicious cycle. Because of joint stiffness or aches and pains, they reduce their activity. But as they move around less, they find that their mobility becomes more and more limited, eventually condemning them to a life on the couch—or the rocking chair. Despite the clear benefits of regular exercise for the elderly, only 37 percent of elderly men and 24 percent of older women exercise regularly (three times a week for 30 minutes or more). According to Dr. Buckwalter, the elderly benefit from aerobic exercise, combined with strength and flexibility training, as well as activities that help to improve balance. He cites a classic study from 1990, "High-Intensity Training in Nonagenarians," where 10 frail women in their late 80s and 90s participated in an eight-week strength training program. By the end of the eight weeks, five of the 10 could walk twice as quickly and two no longer needed canes to walk. Buckwalter concludes, "It wasn't long ago that most people—including physicians—felt that past a certain age, exercise did little good and could do significant harm. Now, however, it has become clear that most older patients benefit substantially from exercise."

Q & A

Question: What is the maximum possible life span of a human being?

Answer: Most researchers feel that 120 years is the maximum, but Ronald Klatz, founder and president of the American Academy of Anti-Aging Medicine, and researcher John C. Wilmoth of University of California at Berkeley believe that the maximum human life span is changing. Dr. Klatz believes people may eventually live 150 years.

MENTAL SHARPNESS

Many people fear declining memory and mental sharpness much more than they fear any of the physical problems that may come with age. Yet there is mounting evidence that memory need not decline as people grow older. What appears to be evidence of memory impairment in some elderly men and women may be the result of depression or come from *assuming* that memory is bound to decline with age. A 2004 study conducted at North Carolina State University reported that, for example, older adults exposed to negative stereotypes about aging did less well on memory tests than those exposed to positive stereotypes. This suggests that the memory loss experienced by some older people may be caused not by changes in the brain but by negative feelings and stereotypes about aging. New research also contradicts an earlier assumption that brain cells do not regenerate. A 1999 Princeton University study reported that adults actually do grow new brain cells throughout life.

Current thinking on memory and mental sharpness in older adults suggests that the "use it or lose it" attitude applies to the brain as well as the body. As with muscles, the brain needs exercise in order to function at its peak. Because physical health and brain health are related, exercise and good nutrition help both the body and the mind. Lawrence C. Katz, a professor of neurobiology at Duke University, suggests what he calls "neurobic" exercises to keep the brain healthy.

The two keys to neurobics are experiencing the unexpected and enlisting the aid of all one's senses during the course of the day. Doing new and challenging things, Katz suggests, creates new pathways in the brain, new connections among nerve cells, and this is what keeps the brain young.

CONNECTEDNESS

Staying connected and involved with others helps the elderly avoid depression. Because being with others provides variety and stimulation, it can also help people stay mentally aware and alive. Also, being with others may help the elderly to be more active. According to the AARP pamphlet, "Staying Sharp," a major public health study involving more than 116,000 people revealed that those who maintained strong relationships had less mental decline and lived more active, pain-free lives without physical limitations. Ideas to help the elderly expand their social networks and combat loneliness include:

- Getting involved with groups and projects
- Taking advantage of community-sponsored programs and senior centers
- Seeking out like-minded people by joining clubs, attending church functions, and volunteering
- Considering the adoption of a pet
- Making friends with people from all different age groups

Many people choose not to retire from their jobs at the so-called retirement age, and others begin new careers after retirement as a way of staying involved with life and expanding their social networks.

In addition to maintaining a healthy lifestyle, challenging the mind, and avoiding isolation, there is one other step the elderly can take in order to ensure successful aging: having a positive view of growing old. A 2002 study published in the *Journal of Personality and Social Psychology,* "Longevity Increased by Positive Self-Perceptions of Aging," found that people who had positive ideas about aging actually lived 7.5 years longer than those who had negative ideas, even when the researchers took into account such factors as age, gender, socioeconomic situation, loneliness, and their health. Just anticipating a healthy happy old age can apparently help guarantee one.

See also: Elderly Men, Aging of; Elderly Women, Aging of; Growing Old in America

FURTHER READING
Rowe, John, M.D., and Robert Kahn, Ph.D. *Successful Aging.* New York: Dell, 1999.

■ LOSS OF A PET

According to the Humane Society, the United States is home to 65 million pet dogs and 77 million pet cats. Because pets have a shorter life span than humans, most pet owners will experience the death of a pet at some time in their lives.

RELATIONSHIPS WITH PETS

In his 1987 book, *The Loving Bond: Companion Animals in the Helping Professions,* Phil Arkow notes that a 14,000-year-old human skeleton was found with hands wrapped around the skeleton of a dog. He views the discovery as indicative of the age and importance of the human-animal bond.

The authors of an article entitled "The Death of a Pet: Implications for Loss and Bereavement Across the Life span," published in the *Journal of Personal & Interpersonal Loss* (2000), maintain that animals today play a larger role in family dynamics than ever before. Because families are smaller today and both parents often work outside the home, young people may spend more time alone than youths in past generations. Therefore, the family pet may be more important in the lives of children today.

Many children describe their pets as their best friends. Bruce Sharkin, author of "Pet Loss: Issues and Implications for the Psychologists," in *Professional Psychology: Research and Practice* (2003), characterizes relationships with pets as "pure," meaning that the bonds are based on unconditional love and acceptance. In their 2002 study about the effect of pets on heart reactivity, K. M. Allen, Jim Blascovich, and W. B. Mendes find that animal companionship can provide people of all ages with a "nonjudgmental" social support that they may not be able to receive from others in their lives.

Many people consider their pets family members. Some pet owners celebrate their pet's birthday, carry pictures of the animal, and confide in their pet. According to Sharkin, a number of studies indicate that animal companionship can have positive effects on people's emotional, social, psychological, and physical well-being. For example, pets can provide a sense of being needed, ease the effects of loneliness, and boost self-esteem. It is not surprising that people grieve at the loss of a pet.

GRIEVING OVER PETS

The death of a pet may be a young person's first experience with death, and the sense of loss may be as deep and abiding as if a family member had died. Since the emotions are similar to those experienced when a person dies, it should be no surprise that the grieving process is similar.

Elisabeth Kübler-Ross's 1969 pioneer work identified the stages of grief that humans experience at the loss of a relative or friend. Those stages also apply to the death of a pet. Kübler-Ross labeled the stages in the grieving process as denial, anger, bargaining, depression, and finally acceptance. For example, immediately after the death of a pet, an owner may have trouble believing that a pet is gone. This stage of disbelief, or denial, may offer the owner emotional protection until he or she is able to internalize the loss of the pet.

Next, the owner may try to pray—or bargain with God—to restore his or her pet to life. Some may feel anger at the pet for dying or turn that anger against anyone who was involved with the pet, including family, friends, and even the veterinarian. Others may feel guilty about what they did or did not do for the pet, or they may believe that it is inappropriate to be as upset as they are over a pet. Depression sometimes accompanies these feelings. Acceptance occurs when the owner accepts the reality of the pet's death. As is the case with the death of a friend or family member, acceptance may be a long time coming.

In some cases, people are faced with the decision of whether or not to euthanize, or "put to sleep," a family pet. In these cases, the grief process may be more difficult and last longer because people feel tremendous guilt at having to make the choice. They may worry that the animal suffered or feel that something more should have been done. In fact, euthanasia, which is accomplished by intravenous injection of a concentrated dose of pain medication, is relatively painless. The animal may feel slight discomfort when the needle pierces the skin, but this sensation is no greater than for any other injection. The solution takes only seconds to induce a total loss of consciousness, which is soon followed by shallow breathing and a stopped heart.

Veterinarians do not take the decision to euthanize a pet lightly. By training, they are oriented toward saving lives, and they are very much aware of the balance between extending an animal's life and ending its suffering. Thus they usually regard euthanasia as a last resort, when they are unable to do anything else to ease the pet's pain. Still, the fact that euthanasia is a kindness to the animal does not keep many owners from feeling profoundly guilty if they must make that choice.

Fact Or Fiction?

It is always a good idea to buy a new pet right away to replace one that has just died.

Fact: While some people may want a new pet right away, others may not. Also, a person cannot replace a pet, and trying to do so may lead to unhappiness and disappointment. If parents buy a new pet for a child before her or she has completed the grieving process, the child may feel guilty and never fully bond with the new pet.

In a 2002 article in *Prevention* magazine, pet expert Arden Moore offers strategies to help recover from the death of a pet, whether the pet was euthanized or died from natural causes. These strategies include:

- Giving yourself permission to grieve
- Seeking out friends and family members who share your compassion for animals
- Treating yourself well, eating nutritious meals, and getting enough sleep and exercise
- Ritualizing your pet's death through a ceremony or memorial service
- Spending time recalling happy memories of times that you shared with your pet
- Considering writing a letter to and from your dead pet

Lorri Green, a licensed psychologist who facilitates pet-loss support groups in California, adds that the healthiest way to honor a pet's memory is to recognize the need to grieve—to feel sadness—so that healing can begin.

Psychotherapist Wallace Sife, in his 1998 book, *The Loss of a Pet*, maintains that pet owners will know that they have reached the stage of acceptance of their pet's death by the following signs:

- They begin to look happier
- They show interest in starting new relationships
- They begin to enjoy doing things that they liked to do before the loss
- They stop feeling guilty for having "good days"
- They allow happy memories to come back along with the sad ones
- They realize and accept the reality of their loss

See also: Grieving, The Process of

FURTHER READING
Arkow, Phillip. *The Loving Bond: Companion Animals in the Helping Professions.* Saratoga, CA: R & E Publishers, Inc., 1987.
Carmack, B. J. *Grieving the Death of a Pet.* Minneapolis, MN: Augsburg Fortress Publishers, 2003.

■ MANAGING DEATH

The idea that one can manage certain aspects of one's death may seem odd—death, almost by definition, seems to strip humans of their last hope of controlling anything. However, since nearly 90 percent of people who die have some warning that death is approaching, the dying have more control than they realize, and many important decisions can be made to ensure what is often referred to as a "good death."

GOOD DEATH

Rutgers University sociology professor Deborah Carr, in an article entitled "A 'Good Death' for Whom? Quality of Spouse's Death and

Psychological Distress among Older Widowed Persons," *Journal of Health and Social Behavior* (2003), writes that most researchers agree a 'good death' consists of end-of-life medical treatment that minimizes avoidable pain and "encompasses important social, psychological, and philosophical elements, such as maintaining close relationships with loved ones during the final days, accepting one's impending death, dying at the end of a long and fulfilling life, and not feeling like a burden to loved ones."

Clearly, the specifics of what constitutes a good death will differ from person to person. In fact, death can be the last full expression of personality and the fitting summing up of a life—if the individual is able to make certain decisions before the final illness. If these decisions are not made in time, however, the dying person may find that he or she has forfeited control to hospitals and medical professionals who focus only on prolonging life—quantity—and not on the quality of the final days.

In order to control the circumstances of their own deaths, many people prepare **advance directives,** a series of legal documents that specify how one wishes to be treated at the end of life. The Patient Self-Determination Act, passed by Congress in 1990, requires that health-care institutions do the following:

- Provide a written summary of the patient's rights to make his/her own health-care decisions

- Provide the institution's policies regarding advance-care directives

- Ask patients if they have advance directives and document the response in the patient's medical record

- Ensure that staff members are educated with respect to advance directives

- Ensure that patients are not discriminated against based on whether or not they have advance directives

Unfortunately, according to the American Medical Directors Association (AMDA), only about 10–15 percent of Americans have advance directives; the remainder may leave their families with the unpleasant task of making many difficult decisions without guidance. There are four types of advance directives:

- A **living will**
- The appointment of a health-care agent

- The appointment of an attorney-in-fact, often called durable power of attorney
- A do-not-resuscitate order (DNR)

A living will is a somewhat detailed statement that indicates what kinds of treatment a person does and does not want if he or she is terminally ill and unable to make decisions for him or herself. A living will may also give family members permission to withdraw life support under certain conditions. A health-care agent is appointed, in writing, to decide whether to withdraw life support if patient is unable to communicate his or her wishes. An attorney-in-fact can make medical decisions other than the withdrawal of life support when the patient cannot. A DNR order may be prepared by the patient, family members, or health-care agents and it, unlike the other kinds of advance directives, must be signed by a doctor. It specifies what, if any, intervention may be used if the patient's heart stops or if he or she stops breathing.

Advance directives are considered necessary in today's society because of technical advances in medicine that can be used to save people suffering from injury and disease who would have surely died only 50–100 years ago. These advances include mechanical ventilation (machines that artificially sustain breathing); cardiopulmonary resuscitation (CPR, a whole complex of interventions to restart a stopped heart, including electric shock and drugs); kidney dialysis; nutritional support and hydration (artificial feeding); and antibiotics. When these procedures are performed on a person in a medical crisis who can return to full functioning, they are invaluable. They can also be beneficial for those who have chronic problems but who can lead relatively normal lives otherwise. Many people with kidney failure can lead productive lives while undergoing dialysis, for example. These same treatments, however, when used in the case of someone with a **terminal illness**, only prolong life and cannot restore it. According to the Partnership for Caring (PFC) in "Talking About Your Choices" (2001), "The success rate [of CPR] is extremely low for people who are at the end of a terminal disease process." Moreover, CPR can be a much rougher procedure than most people think from seeing it enacted on television. It sometimes results in broken ribs and substantial pain and bruising. Additionally, if the heart is not started within a couple of minutes, permanent brain damage may result. According to the PFC, "For the dying patient . . . mechanical ventilation often merely prolongs the dying process until some other body system fails. It may supply oxygen, but it cannot improve the underlying condition."

Thus, individuals who do not want to be subjected to the pain and expense of so-called heroic measures at the end of life must prepare advance directives giving family members and doctors specific directions about what they want and what they do not want. Patients should ensure that copies of all such information are distributed to family members, doctors, and hospitals. It is important to note that advance directives prepared by people under the age of 18 are not legally binding; this means that parents are not obligated to follow the wishes of dying children.

Q & A

Question: What if a person signs a do-not-resuscitate order and then changes his or her mind?

Answer: In such a case, doctors must honor the patient's wishes. Any verbal expression of a change of heart would override the order.

Family members caring for a terminally ill patient at home may not realize that when they call 911 on behalf of the patient, paramedics are obligated by law to resuscitate and transport the patient to the hospital. If the patient does not want such interventions, he or she must keep a copy of a valid DNR order at home.

HOSPICE OR HOSPITAL?

Another aspect of planning one's death should include some thought as to where one would prefer to die. According to the Center for Gerontology and Health Care Research at Brown University, the percentage of those who die in hospitals has decreased dramatically in the last 25 years. In 1989, 61.4 percent of Americans who died of a chronic illness died in an acute care hospital. By 2001, however, fewer than half (49.2) of Americans with chronic illnesses died in the hospital; the remainder died at home or in a nursing home.

Larry H. Goldberg, M.D., in "A Survey of Hospice and Palliative Care," published in *Hospital Physician* (2004), reveals that 80 percent of Americans say they would prefer to die at home but only

Proportion of Deaths Occurring at Home

Percentage of all deaths

☐ 8.0300–13.8200	
▤ 13.8201–17.6300	

⬚ 17.6301–21.2100
■ 21.2101–26.1400

▥ 26.1401–30.5900
▦ 30.5901–32.9400
■ 32.9401–36.4000

Source: Center for Gerontology & Health Care Research, 2001.

about a quarter do so. The reasons for this discrepancy are many, but one reason may be that people are not sufficiently aware of the **hospice** movement, a multifaceted approach to terminal illness that helps families care at home for a dying patient. Also, since 1983, hospice care has been covered by **Medicare** (a federal health insurance program) for eligible patients. Hospice care is based on the idea that there comes a point when continuing to try to cure an illness no longer makes sense and what is needed is **palliative** care, treatment that makes the patient comfortable but no longer attempts to fight the disease. A hospice-care team may include a physician, a nurse, a member of the clergy, physical therapists, social workers, home-health aides, and bereavement coordinators. In order to use hospice care the patient, family, and doctor must agree that the patient has fewer than six months to live. Thus, it is important that advance directives be clear about palliative care, where the patient wants to die, and patients' need to discuss these issues openly with their families.

ORGAN DONATION AND AUTOPSIES

In Belgium, the law assumes that a patient who dies is willing to donate **organs** unless the patient has specifically refused to do so. In the United States, no such assumption is made. After death, family members can choose to donate organs, even if they have never discussed the option with the deceased relative. But they may also refuse to donate organs even if the deceased has signed an organ donor card. Thus it is of crucial importance for families to discuss and agree on this issue before a death occurs.

Fact Or Fiction?

Old people or people who have been very sick cannot donate organs.

Fact: Even those who are quite elderly can donate livers, kidneys, and tissue (corneas, heart valves, bone, skin). If a person dies of a disease, doctors will determine what organs may be usable. The only people who cannot donate any organs or tissue are those diagnosed with HIV. Also, people who do not die in hospitals cannot donate organs because the organs must be removed immediately after death, but tissue can be donated for up to 24 hours after death.

Some people are put off by the idea of an **autopsy**, in which a body is examined **postmortem** to identify the cause of death. Autopsies are required by law in suspicious deaths and homicides and, in some states, if a person dies outside a medical facility. When death is due to natural causes, an autopsy is generally not needed, but physicians or family members may ask for an autopsy if they want to be sure about the cause of death. For those who die as the result of Alzheimer's disease, for example, an autopsy is the only certain method of diagnosis, and families may want to identify the exact nature of the dementia that afflicted their relative. Patients who die of disease may order an autopsy after death if they believe the autopsy can help increase understanding of how a disease progresses or aid in finding a cure.

Many medical researchers are concerned that the rate of autopsies performed in the United States has declined sharply since World War II, from 50 percent then to about 10 percent today. One vocal advocate for doing more autopsies, Stephen A. Geller, chairman of the Department of Pathology and Laboratory Medicine at Cedars-Sinai Medical Center, emphasizes that autopsies provide more than information on the cause of death; they also offer valuable insight into unrecognized disease and the effectiveness of various treatments. According to Geller, there may be as much as a 20 percent discrepancy between doctors' diagnoses and the actual cause of death. "Autopsy is vital to research," Geller adds. "Many important changes in medical care are based on autopsy findings, which translate into improved patient care." As with organ donation, patients who want to have an autopsy performed after death must convey their wishes to family members. It is important for patients and families to know, however, that insurance, except for **Medicare** (a federal health insurance program for people 65 and over and certain disabled people under 65) does not cover autopsies, which can cost from $1,500 to $2,000.

Managing one's own death may restore a sense of control that is seriously threatened by a terminal illness. Advance directives allow the patient to determine his or her own fate in the process and give family members the ability to make tough decisions because they know what their relative wanted.

See also: Death, Unexpected and Planned; Dying, The Process of

FURTHER READING
Albom, Mitch. *Tuesdays with Morrie: An Old Man, A Young Man, and Life's Great Lesson.* New York: Doubleday, 1997.
Webb, Marilyn. *The Good Death: The New American Search to Reshape the End of Life.* New York: Bantam, 1995.

■ MEDIA'S VIEW, THE

How the various news and entertainment media (television, video games, movies, the Internet, newspapers, and magazines) present death and how that presentation affects viewers and readers. Until 125 years ago, the only violence and death that people saw in their entire lives was what they witnessed directly. If a relative died, they were present for the death and viewing. If the local river flooded, local residents dealt with the resulting destruction. If a disaster happened halfway across the country, people could read about it, but they did not see images of it. In fact, the first photograph appeared in a newspaper only in 1880, and many years passed before people began to see images of death and violence in movies and on television.

Thus, although people in the past had a more intimate acquaintance with death than many people do today, an individual, during his or her lifetime, saw only a limited number of images of death. Not so today. Most Americans are bombarded with images of death, some resulting from natural disasters, some resulting from deliberate human actions, and some fictional. Many Americans remember vividly the first live murder ever seen on television, when Dallas strip club owner Jack Ruby shot President John F. Kennedy's accused assassin, Lee Harvey Oswald, as Oswald was being transferred from a city to a county jail, on November 24, 1963. This shocking scene underscored the power of the media to create and amplify a nationwide sense of tragedy and outrage, but it also raised many questions about the responsibility of the media in monitoring the images it transmitted.

THE MEDIA'S PORTRAYAL OF DISASTER AND DEATH

Today there is little that happens of a violent nature anywhere in the world that is not broadcast for all to see. Those who choose to do so, for example, can find on television and on the Internet images of hostages held in Iraq being beheaded by their kidnappers. Newspapers and television programs have broadcast horrific images of the December 2004 tsunami in Southeast Asia, including recognizable images of dead children, eyes open, lying in makeshift morgues. Christian Christensen, a communications professor in Istanbul, Turkey, posted his concerns about media coverage of the tsunami on an Internet site, Common Dreams News Center. He recalls seeing a brief shot of a naked corpse hanging from the branch of a tree. At the time, he was sitting in his living room, drinking coffee. The image convinced him that he was no longer watching news but some perverted form of reality television. How would one feel if that naked boy in the broadcast had been a member of his family? Was it appropriate for such an undignified death to appear as part of a passing spectacle while people had their morning coffee?

Many members of the public remember the image of infant Baylee Almon, bloodied and obviously dead, being carried in the arms of fireman Chris Fields after the bombing of the Alfred P. Murrah Federal Building in Oklahoma City in 1995. That photo won a Pulitzer Prize in 1996, but many people, including Baylee's mother, Aren Almon, found it quite disturbing. Interestingly, however, Ms. Almon later took comfort in the photo—in the image of the gentle hands of the fireman cradling her child—and now has a copy in her home.

Probably the most vivid disaster in the memory of most Americans today is the terrorist attack on the World Trade Center on September 11, 2001. Television news coverage of the events repeatedly showed the planes hitting the buildings and the buildings collapsing. This repetition reached such a point that many viewers feared they would become desensitized to the enormity of the situation by repeated exposure to it.

Q & A

Question: How do journalists who must cover tragedy and disaster cope with what they see and the grief of survivors?

Answer: These kinds of events take a tremendous toll on journalists. The *Daily Oklahoman* provided counseling support for reporters as they worked on the story of the bombing of the Alfred P. Murrah Federal Building in 1995, but many reporters did not take advantage of the opportunity to get help. The newspaper reported that sick leave among reporters rose by 15 percent after the bombing, a fact that seems to indicate that many people working on the story suffered debilitating stress.

Desensitization occurs when a person is exposed repeatedly to something frightening may cause the event to seem less frightening. Desensitization can be a good thing, if, for example, it can help a person overcome an irrational fear. However, desensitization to a disaster of enormous proportions or to violence in general tends not be a good thing, in that people may not react with appropriate human empathy. Bruce D. Perry, an internationally known expert on the effects of trauma on children, notes that as people become desensitized to death or killing, violence increases. A constant environment of killing and strife diminishes the value of human life by decreasing the horror of violent death. People in the United States expose themselves to a remarkable degree of violence. Too many have become desensitized to violent acts, not even realizing the true effects of a bullet passing through a human body.

After 9/11, the *New York Times*, for example, opted to publish photographs of people throwing themselves out of the burning buildings, a decision criticized by many. Psychologists and grief counselors have complained that repeated broadcasting of images of disaster such as what happened on 9/11 can lead to post-traumatic stress disorder, a psychological disorder, among people who lost relatives and friends in disasters. For example, Sandro Galea, a physician at the New York Academy of Medicine who conducted extensive research on the effect of the media on survivors and family members of victims of the 9/11 disaster, has discovered evidence of quite harmful effects from media coverage among survivors.

Over the years, the media has been criticized by many for lack of taste and discretion in the images portrayed to the public. For example, more than 800 people called to complain when the *Press Enterprise*, a newspaper in Riverside, California, published a photo of a dead sheriff's deputy on its front page. However, journalists and publishers defend the use of such images, saying that they fulfill the media's duty to inform the public and inspire people to improve the situations that lead to violence. Marcia McQuern, publisher of the Riverside paper, responded to the public protests against the pictures by saying, "We hoped the picture of the death scene, though bloodless and taken from a distance, would evoke in you, as it did in us, horror at the magnitude of the crime and the loss."

Indeed, many journalists feel strongly that images of disaster have a positive effect. Certainly, there is no question that images of the Southeast Asian tsunami shocked many Americans, but they also spurred numerous relief efforts, as Americans responded with charity, not indifference, to the images of death and destruction. As of January 2005, private donations to help tsunami victims had exceeded $200 million.

According to Rachel Yehuda, professor of psychiatry at Mount Sinai School of Medicine, journalists don't believe that they have any responsibility to look after the mental welfare of the people they report about or report to. Their job—and responsibility—is not that of a mental health worker. The real question is: What is the media's responsibility in general? Yehuda points out that the reason for publishing disturbing images is the important consideration, not the image itself. She notes that images of concentration camp survivors as they were liberated during World War II served to educate the public to the horrific truth about the Nazi regime in Germany. Such images, used for the right reasons, can have the effect of educating viewers, despite being disturbing. Even the depiction of events that are traumatizing can be necessary to allow people to see how bad a situation is and to inaugurate social change.

Many people believe, for example, that media images of the war in Vietnam—the first war to be extensively covered on television—helped to bring about the end of that conflict. Rather than encouraging more violence or desensitization, news coverage actually caused the opposite reaction; people deplored the violence and wanted it to end. Also, after the bombing of the Murrah Federal Building in Oklahoma and 9/11 in New York, Washington, and Pennsylvania, newspapers contributed to the healing of both survivors and the nation as a whole by printing brief biographies of victims. Both the *Daily Oklahoman* and the *New York Times* published photographs and stories that made the victims of their respective disasters more real to people who were struggling to cope with the magnitude of these tragedies and thus put a human face on these events.

THE IMPACT OF MEDIA VIOLENCE
ON REAL-WORLD VIOLENCE

For many years, researchers have expressed concern about the impact of violence in the media on violent behavior in the real world. The question has been repeatedly asked: Does violence as portrayed in the various media lead to an increasingly violent society? The answer increasingly appears to be a qualified "yes," although all researchers acknowledge that the situation is a complicated one. According to psychologist Joanne Cantor, in "The Psychological Effects of Media Violence on Children and Adolescents," a paper presented at the 2002 Colloquium on Television and Violence in Society, such topics are inherently difficult to study. Researchers cannot randomly assign children in early youth to watch different doses of violence on television and then survey them 15 years later to see which of their test subjects committed violent crimes.

Despite such difficulties, most experts who research the impact of violent images on children conclude that there is a link between watching violence and committing violent acts. Some also believe that listening to violent lyrics also has a negative effect on behavior.

Fact Or Fiction?

The only thing parents need to do when it comes to children and televised violence is turn off the set.

Fact: While turning off the TV is often the best solution, clearly it is not always possible or desirable to shield children from violence. Many psychologists emphasize that parents should watch TV with their children and help them to see violence in context, explaining that some of what they see is not real and that other events are unlikely to affect them.

The sheer amount of televised violence that Americans watch is staggering. According to the National Center for Children Exposed to Violence, various studies estimate that the average American has witnessed 200,000 acts of violence on television by the time he or she reaches the age of 18—including 16,000 murders. Moreover, according to a 1999 article "The Impact of Media Violence on Children and Adolescents: Opportunities for Clinical Intervention," American children spend more time watching television than they do attending school. Add to this viewing total the growing amount of violent video games and violent lyrics and music videos, which have not been sufficiently studied, and it becomes clear that American youths are saturated with violent imagery. While some people question the impact of violent imagery on real-world violence, researchers such as Cantor note that statistically, the correlation is nearly as great as that of smoking on lung cancer or the ingestion of lead paint on IQ, and twice as great as the correlation between lack of calcium intake and osteoporosis (weakening of the bones). That is, televised violence is thought to be linked to real-world violence to a greater extent than smoking is to lung cancer.

Craig A. Anderson and Brad J. Bushman, in "The Effects of Media Violence on Society," a 2002 article published in *Science*, note that a variety of kinds of studies—longitudinal (in which people are studied over a period of time), cross-sectional (in which people with very different backgrounds are studied), field (in which people are studied in their natural environments), and laboratory (in which people are given various tests in a laboratory setting)—all indicate a statistically significant link between media and real-world violence. The authors worry that this news is not getting through to lay people from the popular press. In fact, they note that as the scientific community becomes ever more certain that media violence has a negative effect on society as a whole, news reports about the effects of media violence have progressively shifted to weaker statements. What people are hearing is that there is little evidence for such effects.

Most researchers emphasize that violence is a major problem in America and that the media plays a major role in that problem. At the same time, the solutions do not seem to lie with the media, but rather with individuals. Turn off the television, researchers say, and do not allow children to watch repeated images of violence. Write to newspapers that publish disturbing images. Do not buy violent video games or music. Rather than attempting to censor violence, make it unprofitable. That sort of message is hard to ignore.

See also: Violent Death

FURTHER READING
Cantor, Joanne. *Media Violence Alert: Informing Parents about the Number One Health Threat in America Today.* (Parent Education Series #1). Toronto: Dreamcatcher Press, 2000.

■ RIGHT TO DIE, THE

The "right to die" refers to the idea that an individual has the right to choose the time and manner of his or her death. The term is often used interchangeably with euthanasia, or "mercy killing," which itself can be subdivided into a number of categories.

Euthanasia can be "voluntary" or "imposed," depending on whether or not the patient requests the intervention. Imposed euthanasia can be further subdivided into "involuntary" and "non-voluntary." Involuntary euthanasia refers to a situation in which the patient is capable of agreeing to end life but does not do so. Many people, and indeed the law, would call this action murder. Some people might claim that if the victim was in terrible pain and the act was performed with the intention of ending the pain, that it was not, in fact, homicide. Most would disagree strongly.

"Nonvoluntary" euthanasia refers to a situation in which the patient is unable to consent, as with someone who is in a coma. Euthanasia is also further divided into "active" and "passive." Active euthanasia occurs when someone other than the patient assists in the termination of life. "Passive" euthanasia includes ending or withholding treatment, as when a person's feeding tube is disconnected or when a person is removed from a respirator. Physician-assisted suicide (PAS) is a form of voluntary active euthanasia in which a physician provides prescription medication and information about dosage, which the patient can then administer him or herself. Most people today who use the term "right to die" are probably referring to passive euthanasia and PAS.

HISTORY OF THE RIGHT-TO-DIE MOVEMENT

Many people believe that the concept of the right to die is a modern phenomenon, but that is not the case. The Hippocratic Oath, formulated more than 2,000 years ago, tells physicians they must "neither give a deadly drug to anybody if asked for it, nor make a suggestion to this effect." In 1997, Ezekiel Emmanuel, director of the Clinical

Bioethics Department at the National Institutes of Health, published an article in the *Atlantic Monthly* entitled "Whose Right to Die?" He explains that the oath was written at a time when physicians commonly provided euthanasia and assisted suicide for ailments ranging from foot infections and gallstones to cancer and senility.

As the Western world converted to Christianity, the idea that life was sacred began to take hold, and both suicide and euthanasia were no longer accepted as valid methods to end life. In the United States, the modern euthanasia discussion was prompted by advances in anesthesia. In 1870, Samuel Williams proposed that anesthetics be used to end the life of patients in pain. Williams' ideas were discussed nationally over the next 35 years, until a bill to legalize euthanasia was introduced into the Ohio legislature in 1906. Again, a national discussion ensued, even reaching the editorial pages of the *New York Times,* which opposed the idea. The bill was overwhelmingly defeated in the Ohio legislature. In 1938, the Euthanasia Society of America was founded and renamed the Society for the Right to Die in 1974.

The case that brought euthanasia back into the spotlight in the United States was that of Karen Ann Quinlan. Quinlan was just 21 when an overdose of alcohol and tranquilizers left her in a "persistent vegetative state." Although many people used the term *brain dead* to refer to this condition, that term is inaccurate, since a person in a persistent vegetative state still has some brain function. In a persistent vegetative state, the person has lost the higher brain functions (thought, memory, judgment) but retains some of the functions controlled by the brain stem such as breathing, circulation, or movement. A person in a persistent vegetative state may open his or her eyes and may even seem to cry or laugh. Quinlan's parents sued her doctors for the right to remove her from the respirator that doctors said was sustaining her life. They won their case and the court affirmed Quinlan's right to die. After the respirator was removed, however, Quinlan lingered for nearly 10 more years, dying in 1985.

Discussion of the right to die continued in 1978, when Englishman Derek Humphry published a book entitled *Jean's Way,* in which he revealed that he had procured drugs to allow his wife Jean, who was dying of bone cancer, to end her life. While Humphry did not actually administer the drugs, he nevertheless risked a prison sentence because of his assistance to his wife. Questioned by police after the publication of the book, Humphry admitted his guilt but would not name the doctor who had helped him obtain the medicine. He was not prosecuted. Humphry immigrated to the United States, where he founded the Hemlock Society, now called End-of-Life Choices, which advocates for the right to choose one's own method of dying.

In 1984, the Royal Society of Medicine of the Netherlands published its "rules of careful conduct" for euthanasia. Contrary to popular belief, however, the Netherlands did not legalize euthanasia at that time; rather, it declined to prosecute the act if it was performed according to certain guidelines. Not until 2001 was the practice actually legalized.

Q & A

Question: In the Netherlands, what are the circumstances under which euthanasia is permitted?

Answer: The guidelines are as follows:

■ The patient must make an informed and free request and must repeat the request over time.

■ The patient must be experiencing extreme physical or emotional suffering that cannot otherwise be relieved.

■ The attending physician must consult with another, independent physician who concurs that physician-assisted suicide is the only solution.

■ The physician must report the assisted suicide to the coroner.

An Oregon law permitting PAS follows these guidelines and also requires that the patient be over 18, an Oregon resident, have fewer than six months to live, and make three requests for a prescription with at least 15 days between requests. Doctors are required to confirm the terminal diagnosis, ensure that the patient is acting freely, refer the patient to counseling if needed, and inform the patient about hospice care.

In 1986, Roswell Gilbert shot Emily, his wife of 51 years, in the head. He had done so, he said, to end her suffering. Emily had Alzheimer's disease, osteoporosis, and arthritis. She had begged her husband to help her die. Gilbert was arrested for murder and sentenced to life in prison at the age of 75. He was later granted clemency for health reasons.

In 1990, Dr. Jack Kevorkian, a Michigan pathologist, assisted in the suicide of Janet Adkins, who had just been diagnosed with Alzheimer's disease. Kevorkian, nicknamed "Dr. Death" by the media, did what many doctors had done quietly over the years, but he was open, even vocal, about his actions, inviting publicity. He was arrested in Adkins' death, but charges were dropped because Michigan had no laws against suicide or physician-assisted suicide at the time. Laws were subsequently enacted to prohibit the practice, and the state revoked Kevorkian's medical license. Nevertheless, Kevorkian continued to assist in suicides, assisting as many as 120 people in their deaths.

In November 1998, the CBS newsmagazine *60 Minutes* broadcast a video of Kevorkian assisting in the suicide of Thomas Youk, who suffered from a degenerative neurological disease. As a result, the state of Michigan charged Kevorkian with murder. He was convicted and sentenced to 10–25 years in prison. Many in the right-to-die movement hailed Kevorkian as a hero for drawing so much media attention. Others felt that his antics and hunger for publicity made a mockery of the movement.

In 1990, the Supreme Court of the United States upheld the right of a competent person to refuse medical treatment. This decision came in the case of Nancy Cruzan, who was declared to be in a persistent vegetative state as the result of an automobile accident in 1983. Her parents sued to allow her feeding tube to be removed. The Supreme Court concurred but only after its members were convinced that Ms. Cruzan had clearly expressed her preferences before she was injured.

In 1997, the state of Oregon became the only one of the 50 states to legalize PAS. Since the law was enacted, 170 people have died with the assistance of a doctor.

A recently publicized case was that of Terri Schiavo, who was brain-damaged as the result of a heart attack in 1990. For the next 15 years, she was kept alive with a feeding tube. Her doctors declared that she was in a "persistent vegetative state." Her parents, however, disagreed and hired doctors who claimed that Schiavo had some awareness of what was going on around her. When Schiavo's husband petitioned the court to remove the feeding tube, Schiavo's parents fought to keep her alive. In January 2005, the U.S. Supreme Court refused to rule on the constitutionality of a Florida law that

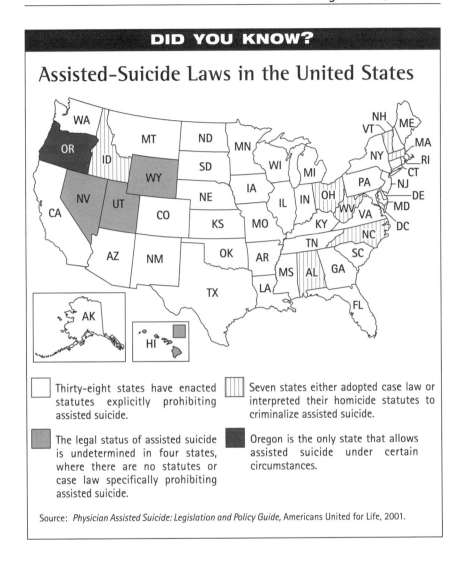

DID YOU KNOW?

Assisted-Suicide Laws in the United States

☐ Thirty-eight states have enacted statutes explicitly prohibiting assisted suicide.

▥ Seven states either adopted case law or interpreted their homicide statutes to criminalize assisted suicide.

▨ The legal status of assisted suicide is undetermined in four states, where there are no statutes or case law specifically prohibiting assisted suicide.

■ Oregon is the only state that allows assisted suicide under certain circumstances.

Source: *Physician Assisted Suicide: Legislation and Policy Guide*, Americans United for Life, 2001.

gave Governor Jeb Bush the power to restore Schiavo's feeding tube. (The Florida Supreme Court had already ruled the law unconstitutional; thus, in effect, the U.S. Supreme Court upheld the lower court's ruling.) Schiavo's parents continued the fight, but the decision of the lower court was affirmed by 19 separate judges. On March 18, 2005, Schiavo's feeding tube was removed for the last time. She died on March 31. The battles to disconnect her feeding tube prompted heated debate over euthanasia and bioethics.

ARGUMENTS FOR EUTHANASIA

Those who support the right to die have four major arguments. First, they believe that determining the time and manner of one's death is a fundamental human right that cannot be taken away by governments. They refer to the idea of a humane death, saying that people should not be forced by the medical profession into a death hooked up to machines in a sterile hospital environment. Secondly, they believe that allowing a person who is in great pain to choose death does more good than harm; that is, they feel that the good that is done by ending the pain overrides the harm of bringing about death. Third, they believe that there is no logical difference between passive euthanasia and active euthanasia. They say the action of removing a feeding tube, which is legal and which many people believe is ethical, is not different in any significant sense from helping a person in pain to end his or her life.

People who support PAS point out that doctors have been quietly helping patients die for many years. According to a 1998 article in the *New England Journal of Medicine*, more than 6 percent of doctors have prescribed lethal drugs when asked by patients. More common yet are medical practices such as "slow code" (deliberately responding slowly to a cardiac or breathing emergency when the patient was terminally ill and had suffered great pain) and giving drugs with "double effect," that is giving a dosage of pain medication that doctors know will not only manage pain but, as a secondary effect, hasten death.

Doctors also routinely withhold treatment when patients have a **do not resuscitate (DNR)** order. This is a legal document that tells doctors not to use heroic measures, such as cardiopulmonary resuscitation (CPR), if there is no reasonable hope of a full recovery. Lastly, those who support euthanasia argue that legalizing it would not cause what some have called "the slippery slope" effect. That is, some opponents of legalizing euthanasia believe it would inevitably lead to killing deformed babies or doing away with the dying just because they are hard to take care of. Those who support the right to die disagree.

Some people who support the right to die, however, take the position that before such a practice is legalized, the entire health-care profession needs to become much more skilled at managing the end of life. They believe, in fact, that if health-care practitioners knew how to manage pain and treat depression among the terminally ill, PAS would not be necessary—or would only be necessary in very rare circumstances. In general, according to Ezekiel Emmanuel's *Atlantic Monthly* article, people who work in hospices, facilities specializing in care for terminal patients, are "deeply opposed to physician-assisted suicide and euthanasia," perhaps because they specialize in managing the pain and depression of the dying and know that the end does not have to be as awful as some fear.

TEENS SPEAK

What Would I Do?

My mom and I were watching TV the other night and there was something on about a woman named Terri Schiavo, who was brain-damaged and being kept alive with a feeding tube. Her husband wanted to remove the feeding tube and let her die, but her parents wanted her to go on living. They were fighting the whole thing out in court.

Anyway, my mom says to me, "Promise, if I am ever in a situation like that, where I don't know what's going on, that you will pull the plug." I could tell she was really serious, but I didn't know what to say. Finally, just to get her off my back, I said "Sure, Ma."

But I really don't know if I could do it. I mean, what if a cure comes along? Or what if there's a chance she could get better? You read about that sometimes when a person is in a coma and then after 10 years suddenly wakes up and asks for breakfast or something.

I would be really scared to make a decision like that. I think even if the doctors said she would never get better, I'd keep on hoping. I wonder if my dad and my brother would feel the same way? Gosh, I just realized my family could have the same kind of fight that the Schiavo family has been having. That's scary.

ARGUMENTS AGAINST EUTHANASIA

The arguments against euthanasia are more complicated than the arguments in favor. Some of the arguments against the practice are religious and philosophical. Some are practical. For example, many with strong religious beliefs oppose euthanasia because they believe that only God should determine the manner and time of death. Some people believe that suffering has spiritual benefits, allowing the individual to grow in both faith and character. Others have more basic concerns; for example, some people fear that if physicians routinely assist in helping patients to die, the trust between patients and doctors will erode, causing irreparable harm to the profession.

Others who argue against euthanasia point out that the reason many people support the practice—the idea of ending unbearable pain—is seldom the reason people choose to end their lives. According to Emmanuel, studies in both the United States and the Netherlands demonstrate that "pain plays a minor role in motivating requests for the procedure." Citing the 1991 Remmelink Report on euthanasia in the Netherlands, Emmanuel reports that "in only 32 percent of all cases did pain play any role in requests for euthanasia; indeed, pain was the sole reason for requesting euthanasia in no cases." The primary reasons for wanting to die included depression, the fear of losing one's dignity, and worry over becoming a burden to family. These conclusions are supported by a Canadian study published in *The Lancet* in 2001. James Lavery of the University of Toronto studied people dying of AIDS. He concluded that three main concerns led people to consider suicide: the fear of losing one's dignity, not wanting to become a burden, and loneliness. These conclusions are also supported by the 2000 annual report on the Oregon Death with Dignity Act published by the Oregon Human Services Department. According to this report, the most frequently reported concerns of those who chose physician-assisted suicide were about losing autonomy and a decreasing ability to participate in activities that made life enjoyable. Few patients cited pain as a primary factor.

Yet another argument against euthansasia is the "slippery slope" theory. Many people fear that once physician-assisted suicide is legalized and people get used to the idea that "mercy killing" is all right in some circumstances, they may become more accepting of euthanizing deformed babies or anyone else who presents a burden to society. Emmanuel says that this trend is, in fact, observable in the Netherlands. He notes that Dutch doctors adhered strictly to the guidelines for euthanasia in only 41 percent of cases and adds that the Remmelink report identifies approximately 1,000 cases a year of nonvoluntary euthanasia, suggesting that perhaps burdensome individuals are being removed. Emmanuel also says that "euthanasia of newborns has been acknowledged. The reported cases have involved babies suffering from well-recognized fatal or severely disabling defects, though the babies were not in fact dying." Emmanuel adds that no one really knows how often such deaths occur; he estimates 10 to 15 cases a year. He concludes that "the Netherlands studies fail to demonstrate that permitting physician-assisted suicide and euthanasia will not lead to the nonvoluntary euthanasia of children, the demented, the mentally ill, the old, and others."

However, the experience in Oregon today would seem to argue against Emmanuel's findings. According to a 2001 article published in the *Journal of the American Medical Association (JAMA)* by Linda Ganzini, M.D., care for terminally ill patients in Oregon has improved since 1994 because doctors have learned more about managing pain and using hospice care.

American have changed their attitudes toward the idea of assisted suicide over the past 50 years, according to Gallup polls conducted in 1950 and 2003. In 1950, only 36 percent of Americans answered "yes" to the question, "When a person has a disease that cannot be cured, do you think doctors should be allowed by law to end the patient's life by some painless means if the patient and his family request it?" In 2003, 72 percent of Americans answered "yes" to the same question. When the question is asked a little differently and includes the word "**suicide**," people answer somewhat differently. To the question, "Regardless of whether or not you think it should be legal, please tell me whether you personally believe that in general doctor-assisted suicide is morally acceptable or morally wrong," 45 percent of respondents to the 2003 Gallup poll answered that the practice was "morally acceptable." On this issue, as on many others, it seems the nation is split.

See also: Doctors' Perspectives; Help and Support; Managing Death

FURTHER READING
Cohen-Almagor, Raphael. *The Right to Die with Dignity: An Argument in Ethics, Medicine, and Law.* New Brunswick, NJ: Rutgers University Press, 2001.
Zucker, Marjory B., ed. *The Right to Die Debate: A Documentary History.* (Primary Documents in American History and Contemporary Issues.) Westport, CT: Greenwood Press, 1999.

■ STAGES OF DEATH, THE

The concept that death is a natural and predictable process that is experienced by the dying person in clearly defined stages was first articulated by physician and expert on the process of dying Elisabeth Kübler-Ross in her 1969 best seller *On Death and Dying.* Kübler-Ross came to her conclusions about dying in the 1950s and 1960s as she watched hospitalized patients try to cope with death in a cold, institutionalized setting. She listened to their stories and began to teach physicians to help people die well instead of simply warehousing and ignoring them.

Kübler-Ross helped to influence the development of the **hospice** movement in the United States. Hospice care, which can be given either at home or in a hospice facility, focuses on caring for people at the end of life. Generally, hospice care involves managing pain, so the dying person can be alert and aware in order to experience the stages of his or her own death, education for the family on what to expect, and nursing help as needed. It rejects the model often seen in hospitals of doing everything possible to prolong the life of a terminal patient, no matter how painful or invasive.

Q & A

Question: Did Elisabeth Kübler-Ross create the hospice concept?

Answer: The first hospice was founded in England by Dame Cicely Saunders, a physician who began working with the dying in the 1940s. Saunders founded St. Christopher's Hospice in London. She defined the mission of the hospice movement when she said, "We do not have to cure to heal." The first American hospice, the Connecticut Hospice, opened in 1974.

PSYCHOLOGICAL STAGES OF DEATH

Kübler-Ross suggested that people who do not die suddenly pass through five psychological stages in preparation for their own deaths. These stages are denial, anger, bargaining, depression, and, finally, acceptance. In the denial stage, people refuse to accept what is happening to them. They may seek treatments even when they have been told that nothing can be done. The person is in a state of shock. Next comes anger. People may become angry at their doctors, their friends and family, and even at themselves. Sometimes people become angry at others just because they are healthy and their lives will go on. After anger comes bargaining. Those who believe in God may pray, "If only You will allow me to live, I promise I'll spend less time at work." Those who are not religious may bargain with themselves: "If I live, I'll never lose my temper again." Depression is the next stage, as people begin to accept the inevitable and to believe that they will, in fact, die. Many dying people withdraw from friends and family at this stage and may even feel guilty at causing family members pain. The final stage is acceptance. The person gives up fighting and accepts the inevitability of his or her own mortality.

Throughout all the stages, Kübler-Ross says, hope weaves its way in. Even in the midst of depression, for example, a dying person may begin to hope for a cure or a reprieve. It is also important to remember that these stages do not occur in exactly the same way for everyone, nor does one automatically follow the other. People may move back and forth and skip stages.

Critics of Kübler-Ross have complained that her model is rigid and appears to tell people how they should progress toward death instead of reflecting the various ways different people come to accept their impending mortality. One such critic, Joan Retsinos, a professor at Brown University, points out that Kübler-Ross's work was based on middle-aged cancer patients. These patients, Retsinos believes, may not view death the same way as teenagers or elderly people. She suggests, for example, that the elderly may not be as likely to "deny" what is happening to their bodies.

If Kübler-Ross's theory about the stages of death is imperfect, it has nevertheless helped many family members cope in a more productive way with the deaths of those they love. For example, family members who understand that anger is normal can be more supportive of the dying person and allow him or her to express anger and despair.

In fact, Dr. Charles A. Corr, in a 1993 article in *Death Studies*, emphasizes that the most valuable lessons to be learned from Kübler-Ross's work are not for the dying but for family members who will live on. These lessons are:

- Assisting the dying person in resolving unfinished needs
- Actively listening to the dying person

- Helping the dying person to identify his or her own needs

- Learning from the dying person in order to come to know one's self better

PHYSICAL DEATH

Dying is a physical as well as a psychological process. Signs that the body is shutting down include:

- Sleeping most of the time

- Cool, moist skin that takes on a purplish color

- Rasping sounds in breathing (sometimes called the "death rattle")

- Rhythmic periods (lasting for seconds) of not breathing (apnea)

Family members frequently wonder if the dying person hears them or is aware of their presence. Although no one knows, some people believe that the dying person has a more expanded awareness than physical senses allow. Since no one knows for sure, it certainly cannot hurt to talk to your dying friend or relative and to say things such as "I love you" or "I'll miss you." Certainly such expressions of feeling help the living, even if the dying cannot hear.

Death, as a physical process, also happens in stages. Stephen J. Spignesi, *The Odd Index*, explains the stages in which the body processes gradually stop.

At the moment of death:

- The heart stops beating.

- The muscles relax.

- The bladder and bowels empty.

- Body temperature begins to drop one and one-half degrees Fahrenheit per hour.

After 30 minutes:

- Pale color increases.

- Feet and hands turn blue.

- Eyes sink back into the skull.

After four hours:

■ Stiffness, or rigor mortis, sets in and continues for about 24 hours.

See also: Grieving, The Process of

FURTHER READING
Kübler-Ross, Elisabeth. *Death and Dying.* Reprint, New York: Scribner, 1997.
Nuland, Sherwin B. *How We Die: Reflections on Life's Final Chapter.* New York: Vintage, 1995.

■ TEENAGE DEATHS

Perhaps the most important thing to know is that nearly *all* teenage deaths are preventable. In 2002, the three primary causes of death among young people ages 15–24 were, in descending order: unintentional injuries (including automobile crashes), suicide, and homicide. Alcohol and drug use were often contributing factors in these deaths.

ACCIDENTS

According to the National Center for Injury Prevention and Control (NCICP) publication "Teen Drivers: Fact Sheet," approximately 5,000 teenagers die in car accidents each year in the United States. Per mile driven, teenagers are four times more likely than any other group, including the elderly, to be involved in a crash. Teenagers, although they represent only about 10 percent of the U.S. population, account for 14 percent of motor vehicle fatalities. The more passengers there are in a car with a teen driver, the higher the risk of an accident. In 2002, the cost to the American economy of all automobile crashes among teenagers, fatal and nonfatal, was $40.8 billion. Boys are twice as likely as girls to have fatal accidents.

The reasons for this high rate of automobile crashes among teens are many. According to the NCICP, lack of experience is a key factor, as is underestimating risk in situations such as running red lights, making illegal turns, and riding with someone who has had too much to drink. Nearly 30 percent of all the teen drivers who died in automobile accidents had, themselves, been drinking. Moreover, teenagers

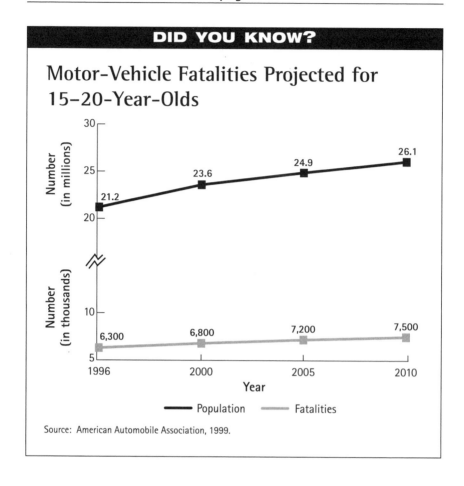

DID YOU KNOW?

Motor-Vehicle Fatalities Projected for 15–20-Year-Olds

Source: American Automobile Association, 1999.

are less likely than other age groups to wear seat belts. The Centers for Disease Control and Prevention's 2002 Youth Risk Behavior Surveillance System survey found that as many as 14 percent of high school students rarely or never wear seat belts. Again, males were significantly less likely than females to wear seat belts.

Many states have adopted stricter driving laws for teenagers, sometimes called "Graduated Driver Licensing" or GDL. In most cases, these laws restrict a young driver's privileges until he or she has demonstrated safe driving habits. These laws also include tougher penalties for violations. Graduated license laws may limit how many passengers may be in the car with a teenage driver and may restrict driving between certain hours, in many cases between midnight and five A.M. In 2002, the Substance Abuse and Mental Health Services Administration reported that fewer teenagers drink and drive in states that have restrictive licensing laws. In the most restrictive states, 8.2 percent of teen drivers reported driving under the influence, as opposed to 11.5 percent in the least restrictive. Teenagers themselves can prevent many accidents by reducing distractions (including other passengers, music, and cell phones), wearing seat belts, and never drinking and driving or riding with someone who has been drinking.

SUICIDE

According to the Centers for Disease Control and Prevention's Web-based Injury Statistics Query and Reporting System, approximately 2,000 teenagers kill themselves each year. The CDC also reports, in a survey conducted in 2000, that one in five teenagers had thought about suicide, one in six had gone so far as to make plans to commit suicide, and one in 12 had attempted suicide in the prior year. To put these figures in perspective, the National Youth Violence Prevention Resource Center, in "Facts for Teens: Teen Suicide," states that in a class of 25 students, at least five are likely to have seriously considered suicide, and at least two are likely to have tried to kill themselves in the past year. Females are nine times more likely to attempt suicide than males, but males are four times more likely to actually kill themselves. Females tend to use pills in their suicide attempts; males typically use firearms. Overall, guns are used in more than 60 percent of teen suicides.

TEENS SPEAK

It Almost Happened to Me

Last year, things just seemed overwhelming: SATs, college choices, schoolwork, and then I broke up with my boyfriend—we'd been dating since freshman year. I lost it. I cried all the time. I could hardly drag myself out of bed in the morning, and, of course, my grades started to drop. I didn't care about my makeup or my hair or what I wore any more.

My mom kept yelling at me about how sloppy I looked. Then I watched a show on TV about a girl my age who killed herself, and the idea began to seem very comforting. So I went to my mom's medicine cabinet and swallowed a whole handful of pills. The next thing I knew, I was in the hospital with all kinds of tubes hanging off me—and my mom looked awful. She'd been up all night sitting with me and crying. Well, it turned out that I was what they call "clinically depressed" (not just sad but depressed enough that I needed medical help). I saw a therapist, and she put me on medication. I feel great now and just got accepted to college. I even have a new boyfriend. I am so glad I didn't die.

According to the National Center for Health Statistics, the rate of teen suicide nearly doubled in the 20 years between 1970 and 1990. Since then, the rate has stabilized at about 11 deaths per 100,000 young people.

"Facts for Teens: Teen Suicides," outlines six factors that increase the likelihood that an individual will commit suicide:

- A previous attempt. As many as one third of those who commit suicide have made a previous attempt.

- Depression. Perhaps as many as one in four teenagers suffer from treatable depression. While not all depressed teens commit suicide, depression is a significant factor in most suicides.

- Substance abuse. Alcohol and many drugs have a depressive effect on the brain and they interfere with a person's ability to make good decisions. Drugs and alcohol are factors in many suicides and suicide attempts.

- Family history of suicide. Many teens who kill themselves have a relative who attempted or committed suicide. Depression and other mental illnesses have been shown to have a genetic component.

- Stress. When someone is already depressed, stresses, such as doing poorly on a test or breaking up with a boyfriend or girlfriend, may become overwhelming.

- Access to guns. Since so many teens use guns to kill themselves, limiting access would prevent many deaths.

- Other suicides. Teens may be influenced to commit suicide if they have heard about recent suicide attempts by other teenagers.

Not all suicides can be prevented, and the parents and friends of a teen who kills him or herself should not blame themselves. However, learning to recognize the warning signs can prevent many such deaths. Teens should always tell a trusted adult if they suspect a friend might be thinking about suicide, even if they have been sworn to secrecy. Parents and other adults in a teen's life should pay attention to these warning signs:

- Withdrawal from family and friends

- Inability to concentrate or think clearly

- Changes in eating or sleeping habits

- Neglecting one's appearance

- Talk about hopelessness, suicide, "getting away," or death

- Any kind of self-destructive behavior (drinking, driving too fast, etc.)

- Loss of interest in favorite activities

- Giving away prized possessions

- Sudden happiness after a period of depression (which can indicate that the person has decided to kill him or herself and feels relieved that the decision has been made)

Many suicides are impulsive acts, made in a moment of intense sadness, and many take place while under the influence of alcohol or drugs, which seriously impair judgment. Teens go through dramatic ups and downs as they make their way to maturity. Often with help from supportive adults, teens who consider suicide can find their way to happiness again.

HOMICIDE

According to the U.S. Department of Justice's *Juvenile Justice Bulletin* of October 2001, nearly 1,800 teenagers were victims of homicide in

1999. This translates into five murders a day, making the United States the most deadly of all developed nations for teens. The rate of juvenile homicide in the United States is five times higher than that of 25 other developed countries combined. Only unintentional injuries and suicide kill more teens than homicide.

Eighty-one percent of teen homicide victims are male and 52 percent are minorities. Most such deaths occur in urban areas; in fact, most occur in just five cities: Chicago, Detroit, Philadelphia, Los Angeles, and New York. Some states, such as Nevada, Illinois, Louisiana, Maryland, and Alaska, have relatively high rates of juvenile homicide (five to six per 100,000 of population), and some states, such as New Hampshire, South Dakota, Wyoming, Montana, North Dakota, and Kansas have low rates (one or fewer per 100,000 of population). Guns are the weapon of choice in 86 percent of all teen homicides, and for every gun death, there are four self-inflicted injuries.

Fact Or Fiction?

Teen homicides have been continually increasing over the last 20 years.

Fact: Even though the United States has the highest teen homicide rate of any developed country today, it is much improved since 1993, when 2,880 teenagers were murdered. Between 1984 and 1993, teenage homicides increased 158 percent and then began to decline, reaching a 21-year low in 2001.

According to "Children, Youth, and Gun Violence: Analysis and Recommendations," published in *The Future of Children* (2002), "No single policy solution will end youth gun violence in the United States; a wide repertoire of approaches is needed to address different aspects of the problem." Crucial interventions include:

- Reducing exposure to guns. Keeping young people away from guns is the single most important strategy. Parents should get rid of guns in the home or, if they must keep guns, be sure they are securely stored. Parents should also ensure that the families of their children's friends take the same precautions. In addition, parents should monitor children's exposure to media violence.

- Educating parents. Because several studies conclude that educating children and adolescents to stay away from guns does not seem to have much impact on their behavior, educating parents is the next-best option: "It is critical that parents understand the risks that guns pose to their children."

- Community intervention. Many young people carry guns in urban areas because they do not feel safe without a gun. Leaders must find ways to make their communities safer places to live and work.

- Stronger law enforcement. Police need to aggressively enforce laws against gun possession by youths. They also need to actively prosecute those who sell illegal firearms to teens.

- Change the design of guns. Child safety grips and easy-to-see indicators that a gun is loaded are two changes that could help prevent gun violence. "Smart guns" that will only fire when they recognize the gun owner's thumbprint could prevent both intentional and unintentional shootings. As is the case with unintentional injuries and suicide, many homicides involving teens can be prevented and hundreds of young lives saved.

See also: Attitudes Toward Death, Teenage; Terminal Diseases Affecting Youths; Violent Death

FURTHER READING
Empfield, Maureen and Nicholas Bakalar. *Understanding Teen Depression: A Guide to Diagnosis, Treatment, and Management.* New York: Owl Books, 2001.

■ TERMINAL DISEASES AFFECTING YOUTHS
Although the three leading causes of death among people ages 15–24 are unintentional injuries, suicides, and homicide, disease also takes its toll. According to a 2001 report from the organization Children's Hospice International, between 75,000 and 100,000 children with

terminal diseases die each year in the United States. The primary disease-related causes of death among young people are certain forms of cancer and congenital heart disease, that is, heart disease that was present from birth. Diabetes, while it causes fewer deaths, ranks as a major health problem for many young people.

CANCER AMONG ADOLESCENTS

Cancer describes many diseases that have one thing in common—cells in the body grow abnormally and out of control. Over time, these cells spread throughout the body and destroy normal tissue in various organs, making the person with cancer very sick. Chemotherapy, anticancer drugs that are usually administered intravenously, or directly into the veins, is used to destroy cancerous cells. Frequently, chemotherapy has side effects of nausea, fatigue, and hair loss.

In 2001, according to the National Cancer Institute, 8,600 children were diagnosed with cancer and 1,500 died, making cancer the leading disease-related cause of death among children. About one-third of the cancers are forms of leukemia, or cancer of the blood. The five-year survival rates for all childhood cancers have improved dramatically in the last 20 years. While in 1974-76 only 55.7 percent of children diagnosed with cancer survived, between 1992 and 1997, the survival rate was 77.1 percent.

There are four other forms of cancer that tend to attack adolescents. Osteosarcoma is a type of bone cancer that appears most often in teenage boys during periods of rapid growth. It tends to be found in people who are taller than average. Symptoms of osteosarcoma are pain and swelling, usually in an arm or leg; sometimes a lump appears at the site of the pain. To treat this form of cancer, doctors usually prescribe surgery to remove the tumor, then chemotherapy. Sometimes doctors are able to remove just the tumor and surrounding tissue, but if the tumor has metastasized, or spread to nearby tissue, then doctors have no choice but to amputate the limb. According to Robert Grimer, an orthopedic oncologist in Birmingham, England, only 54 percent of patients with osteosarcomas survive more than five years. He adds that treatments have not improved during the past 20 years. Chemotherapy and removing part or all of the affected limb are still the standard therapies available. Grimer believes that there is an urgent need for new treatments to be developed that are more effective, but kinder to the patients themselves.

DID YOU KNOW?

Leading Causes of Death, 2001

Developing Countries	Number of Deaths	Developed Countries	Number of Deaths
1. HIV/AIDS	2,678,000	1. Ischemic heart disease	3,512,000
2. Lower respiratory infections	2,643,000	2. Cerebrovascular disease	3,346,000
3. Ischemic heart disease	2,484,000	3. Chronic obstructive pulmonary disease	1,829,000
4. Diarrheal diseases	1,793 000	4. Lower respiratory infections	1,180,000
5. Cerebrovascular disease	1,381,000	5. Trachea/bronchus/lung cancers	938,000
6. Childhood diseases	1,217,000	6. Road traffic accidents	669,000
7. Malaria	1,103,000	7. Stomach cancer	657,000
8. Tuberculosis	1,021,000	8. Hypertensive heart disease	635,000
9. Chronic obstructive pulmonary disease	748,000	9. Tuberculosis	571,000
10. Measles	674,000	10. Self-inflicted	499,000

Source: WHO. *World Health Report*, 2001.

Ewing's sarcoma is another kind of bone cancer that affects teenagers. Ewing's sarcoma is very similar to osteosarcoma in its symptoms and treatment, though it differs in sometimes being found in the pelvis or hip bone. The outlook for Ewing's sarcoma patients is similar to those with osteosarcoma. According to St. Jude's Children's Research Hospital, about 60 percent of sufferers whose tumors have not spread survive; for those whose tumors have metastasized, the survival rate is only about 30 percent.

Leukemia is another cancer that is common in children and adolescents. It occurs when abnormal white blood cells get into the bone marrow and the bloodstream. When this happens, the person afflicted with leukemia cannot fight infections effectively. As the white blood cells multiply, they interfere with the body's ability to produce red blood cells that carry oxygen around the body. Symptoms of leukemia include frequent infections, bleeding, and anemia, a condition of the blood resulting from too few red blood cells. The survival rate for children with the most common form of leukemia (acute lymphocytic leukemia) is 85 percent, according to the American Cancer Society.

TEENS SPEAK

I Had a Brain Tumor When I Was 16

I was only 16 when I was diagnosed with a neuroblastoma, which is a kind of tumor. Mine was in my brain. I had terrible headaches that got so bad I couldn't see, and then I started fainting. That's when my mom took me to the doctor.

I had to have surgery to get rid of the tumor and then radiation to get the rest of the cancer out of my body. Afterward, I looked awful. I lost a whole lot of weight and all my hair, then I got scaly red patches all over my skin.

A lot of people from school were really uncomfortable around me because I looked so bad, I guess. But a few of my friends stuck by me, including my girlfriend, Liz. The thing I hated most is that strangers would stare at me and that just reminded me how bad I looked.

I'm 18 now and doing well, but my hair will probably never grow back, so I wear a lot of baseball caps. I missed graduating with my class, but I will graduate from high school this year and go on to college next year.

Lymphomas are cancers of the lymphatic system, which is a collection of organs that helps to protect the body from disease. Lymph nodes, bone marrow, the thymus gland, and the spleen are parts of the lymphatic system. Two kinds of cancers affect the lymph system: Hodgkin's disease and non-Hodgkin's lymphoma. Hodgkin's disease is characterized by large cells called Reed-Sternberg cells and is a cancer of lymph tissue. Non-Hodgkin's lymphoma is similar to leukemia in that it involves cancerous white blood cells. Both diseases manifest similar symptoms, which include swollen lymph nodes in the upper body, usually in the neck, collarbone region or armpits. Sometimes swelling occurs in the groin. These swollen nodes are usually painless. Flu-like symptoms including fever may also signal a lymphatic cancer, and many patients report itching and unexplained weight loss. It is important to note, however, that there are many conditions—most of them norcancerous—that can cause swollen lymph nodes, especially in children. A lymph node that returns to normal size within a few weeks is probably not cancerous. Hodgkin's disease is usually treated with chemotherapy; patients with non-Hodgkin's lymphoma may also require radiation treatments. According to the Pediatric Oncology Resource Center, about 60 percent of those with non-Hodgkin's lymphoma and as many as 75 percent of those with Hodgkin's survive the disease.

ADOLESCENTS WITH HEART DISEASE

There are two kinds of heart disease that affect children, congenital and acquired. The most common of these diseases is congenital—victims are born with it. According to the American Heart Association, about 40,000 children are born each year with heart defects, including heart valve defects and defects in the walls that separate the chambers of the heart. Some cases of congenital heart disease are genetic. Others may be caused by the mother's alcohol or drug abuse during pregnancy, while still others may be caused by maternal viral infections, including German measles. Cases of congenital heart disease may be detected in infancy; others may not be discovered until many years later. Symptoms of heart disease include shortness of breath and difficulty in exercising.

Many congenital heart defects can be corrected by surgery, but individuals with congenital heart defects, even if they have been corrected, may still be vulnerable to endocarditis, which is an inflammation of the inside of the heart. Endocarditis is an acquired condition that is caused when bacteria enter the bloodstream. It is not uncommon for bacteria to enter the bloodstream, and the body can usually fight off infection. However, if the heart is damaged, bacteria can attach to the lining of the heart and from there spread infection to other parts of the body. Certain medical procedures can cause endocarditis, including surgical removal of the adenoids or tonsils and dental cleanings. People who have congenital heart damage can help to prevent endocarditis by taking antibiotics before such procedures.

According to a 2003 report in *Pediatric Infections Disease Journal*, body piercings and tattooing may also cause the disease. Abuse of any drug that requires an injection can also cause endocarditis.

Endocarditis is sometimes hard to diagnose. Symptoms include chills, cough, fever, fatigue, muscle aches, and joint pain. Untreated, endocarditis can lead to heart attack, heart failure, and stroke. Treatment for endocarditis involves the administration of intravenous antibiotics over a six-week period. Surgical replacement of damaged heart valves may also be required.

DIABETES

Diabetes is a chronic disease that is characterized by the body's failure to properly use or make the hormone insulin, which is needed to store or use glucose, or blood sugar. Diabetes manifests itself as one or two major types. In type 1 diabetes, referred to as juvenile or insulin-dependent diabetes, the body is unable to produce insulin. Type I diabetes mainly occurs in children and adolescents 18 years and younger. According to the National Institutes of Heath, there are 206,000 diabetes sufferers under the age of 20 in the United States. Although Type 1 diabetes accounts for only .6 percent of teenage deaths, it is the sixth-leading cause of death in the United States overall, and the death rate of middle-age people with diabetes is twice that of those who do not have the disease.

In type 2 diabetes, referred to as adult-onset or non-insulin-dependent diabetes, the body is unable to use the limited amount of insulin that it produces. Type 2 diabetes historically occured in adults over 30 years of age but is now epidemic among teenagers.

According to the government initiative Healthy People 2010, approximately 800,000 new cases of diabetes are diagnosed each year in America, or 2,200 per day. More than half of the 10.5 million people with diabetes are undiagnosed because they do not yet exhibit symptoms.

Youth is usually a time associated with tremendous health and vitality. The idea that any disease can cut a young life short surprises and shocks many people. There are a number of medical conditions that can damage health and even kill young patients. Treatments do exist, however, offering cures or at least prolonged life for sufferers.

See also: Attitudes Toward Death, Teenage

FURTHER READING
McAuliffe, A. *Growing up with Diabetes: What Children Want Their Parents to Know.* New York: John Wiley & Sons, 1998.

■ TRADITIONS AND DEATH

According to an early authority on death rituals, Bertram S. Puckle, in his landmark 1926 study *Funeral Customs: Their Origin and Development*, most funeral traditions arose because early humans feared death and the spirit of the deceased, which they believed death had set loose from the body. Such spirits returned to their old surroundings with terrible supernatural powers, against which the living had no protection. Living people had to take elaborate precautions against vengeful ghosts.

Thus, many traditions associated with funerals in America today originated thousands of years ago, and we often follow these traditions without really understanding their original intent.

WHY DO WE . . . ?

One Western funeral custom that most people are familiar with is wearing black to signify mourning. Other cultures wear different colors. Most Chinese wear white, the Burmese wear yellow, South Africans red, and the Turks violet. The idea of wearing particular clothing to signify mourning goes back to the idea that one must hide from the spirit of the dead person or from the spirits that come to fetch the dead person's soul. In some cultures, people may cover their faces with veils or paint or even mask themselves in order to fool the spirits.

The wearing of elaborate mourning garb reached its height in England and America during the Victorian era, named after Queen Victoria of England, who reigned from 1837 to 1901. In 1861, Victoria's beloved husband, Prince Albert, died; she was so devastated that she wore mourning clothes for the rest of her life and began a fashion that included rigid rules about what to wear and for how long. This fashion applied most strictly to women whose husbands had died. These clothes, called widow's weeds ("weeds" is an old word for clothing), were intended to signal that a woman was in intense mourning and was, hence, off-limits as a prospective bride for at least two to three years.

The rituals surrounding how one wore mourning clothes included several stages. The first was set at a year and a day. During this period, the widow would not leave the house without a long black veil over her face. Indoors, she wore a cap trimmed in black, called a widow's cap. Her garments were to be entirely black, made of dull fabrics, and ornamentation such as jewelry had to be made of jet, a black stone that is a hard, dark variety of coal. Even the petticoat had to have a black ribbon run along the hem.

For the next nine months, the rules were relaxed a bit, allowing for the veil to be lifted from the face and some forms of ornamentation, such as flowers and ribbons, to be added. The third stage, called half-mourning, allowed some dark colors, such as gray, purple, and mauve, to be added to the wardrobe, and jewelry could be worn. Today, most people confine themselves to wearing dark colors on the day of the funeral.

Other funeral customs that originated from fear include:

- Lighting candles. Early humans believed that fire could protect them and the deceased from evil spirits. Later, it was thought that light was necessary to guide the soul to its eternal resting place. The word *funeral* comes from the Latin for "torch."

- Ringing bells/firing rifles. Noise was believed to frighten off evil spirits. Funeral music may have originated from ancient chants designed to please the spirits.

- Wakes. Sitting up all night with a corpse was a way of protecting the body from evil spirits and of ensuring that the person was actually dead, as people had a great fear of being buried alive. This custom evolved into the viewing at a funeral home as it is practiced in America today.

Just as some funeral customs arose from fear, others arose from the belief that the deceased person might need help on the way to the afterlife or require material possessions when he or she got there. Archeologists have discovered graves of Neanderthal people dating back 60,000 years, which contained evidence of people being buried with gifts. Objects such as flowers and antlers have been found with bodies, which were carefully placed within graves, often posed to look as if they were sleeping on their sides.

The practice of sending material possessions with the deceased may have reached its pinnacle in ancient Egypt, where many elaborate funeral practices were designed to help the dead person in the afterlife. Embalming, the prevention of body decomposition through the use of chemical processes, was practiced because the Egyptians believed that the body had to be intact in order to fully participate in the afterlife. This belief also motivated the constructions of **sarcophagi**, stone coffins and tombs to protect the remains, as well as offerings of food and drink and precious objects. Sometimes servants were buried with their masters, but this practice was eventually ended and the actual servants were replaced with replicas or drawings.

Other cultures also practiced the custom of burying gifts and even other people with the dead. Ancient Incans were buried with their most prized possessions and servants. The practice of **suttee** involved widows in some parts of India being immolated, or sacrificed, in the flames from their husbands' funeral **pyres**. This practice also occurred in ancient Egypt, China, and Scandinavia. The original purpose of suttee was probably to ensure that the couple would be reunited in the afterlife.

Fact Or Fiction?

Indian widows who committed suttee by joining their husbands on the funeral pyre did so voluntarily.

Fact: Some did so voluntarily, believing they would guarantee respect and honor to their families. But others were forced by family members and loud music had to be played to drown their screams. Some women who appeared to go voluntarily were actually drugged.

The modern equivalent of the custom of burying the dead with gifts are the flowers sent by friends and relatives and the donations to charity made in the name of the deceased. In place of the gifts of food that were once made to the deceased, we now bring food to the family and often return to the home of the deceased after the funeral to eat. People still bury relatives with prized possessions, such as wedding rings, and children are sometimes buried with toys.

CUSTOMS AROUND THE WORLD

There are three elements that nearly all cultures and religions have in common when it comes to dealing with the dead. These are:

- Rituals or ceremonies to mark the death
- A sacred place to dispose of the body
- Customs to help remember the deceased

In nearly every culture, the body is handled with respect after death, washed to remove impurities, and covered with a cloth called a shroud. Some religions require the anointing of the body with particular oils or the burning of incense or fragrant woods. Many religions have particular prayers that are required. Jews say the mourner's Kaddish, which begins, "May His great Name grow exalted in the world that He created as He willed." Muslims turn the body to face Mecca and pray *salatul janazah*, or funeral prayers. Buddhists recite holy prayers called sutras and spend three days watching over the body.

Q & A

Question: Why are pallbearers called that? What is a pall?

Answer: Pallbearers are those who carry the casket to the grave. The name comes from ancient Rome, where the body of a dead person was covered with a cloak, called a *pallium*. Over the centuries, the word was shortened to "pall," and the cloak became a rectangular cloth for covering the coffin. As the coffin was carried to the grave-yard, those who were doing the actual carrying were accompanied by others who held on to the pall to keep it from blowing away. Some reli-gions still use a pall to cover a casket while it is in a church; in military funerals, the nation's flag replaces the pall.

Burial in the ground or in chambers above the ground and crema-tion are the two most common methods for disposing of human remains, and in most religions, the place where these ceremonies occur is considered sacred. Jews and Muslims require that the body be interred as soon as possible. Muslims bury a body directly in the ground, so decomposition will take place quickly. Many Jews require that the dead be buried in a plain coffin, usually a plain box made of inexpensive wood, that is wide at shoulder level and narrow at the bot-tom. Some cultures, however, choose to leave the body exposed. Australian aborigines left bodies in trees. People of the Solomon Islands left bodies on reefs for sharks to eat. To this day, the Parsis of India (people of the Zoroastrian faith, followers of the prophet Zarathustra) dispose of the dead by leaving the corpse on a tower to be devoured by vultures. Parsis believe that burying a body in the earth pollutes the land, and they believe fire is too sacred to use for such a task.

There are many different ways to help the living continue to remember the dead. Tombstones and urns to hold the ashes of the deceased fill this function, as do memorials or holy cards, printed with the deceased person's birth and death information. Jews celebrate the first anniversary of death by unveiling the gravestone. In many cul-tures, people visit cemeteries on death anniversaries and holidays to place flowers and wreathes on graves. Perhaps the most elaborate memorial ritual is the Mexican Día de los Muertos, or Day of the Dead, celebrated on November first and second. This tradition, which can be traced to the ancient Aztecs, is a joyous celebration of life as well as a way of remembering the dead. People visit cemetaries, where they decorate relatives' graves and have a picnic, and they also set up altars in their homes decorated with brightly colored flowers. They may also set a place for the deceased at the dinner table and eat candy in the shape of skeletons and a special bread called *pan de muerto*, or "bread of the dead."

Sir William Gladstone, prime minister of England from 1868 to 1894, once said, "Show me the manner in which a nation cares for its dead, and I will measure with mathematical exactness the tender mercies of its people, their respect for the laws of the land, and their loyalty to high ideas." Gladstone made clear that funeral traditions in general, whatever their nature, are indicative of the respect a people have for human life.

See also: Cremation; Grieving, The Process of

FURTHER READING

Puckle, Bertram S. *Funeral Customs: Their Origins and Development.* 1926. Reprint, Holmes, PA: Omnigraphics, 1990.

Rogak, Lisa. *Death Warmed Over: Funeral Food, Rituals and Customs from Around the World.* Berkeley, CA: Ten Speed Press, 2004.

■ VIOLENT DEATH

Loss of life due to the use of physical force is considered "violent death." According to the Centers for Disease Control and Prevention (CDC) violent death "results from the intentional use of physical force or power, threatened or actual, against oneself, another person, or a group or community." Examples of violent deaths include homicides and suicides. The death of a loved one is among the most difficult events anyone can face. However, when that person dies violently, families suffer to a much greater extent.

STATISTICS OF VIOLENT DEATH

The CDC reports that approximately 50,000 people die violent deaths each year in the United States; 60 percent of those who die violently commit suicide, and 40 percent are murdered. In 2002, 17,600 people died of homicide.

In 2001, homicide was the second-leading cause of death among teenagers and young adults, ages 15–24. Approximately 14 people in this age group die violently each day in the United States.

According to Dr. Etienne Krug of the CDC, American children are more likely to die from homicide than children in 25 other industrialized countries. "Our children are getting killed . . . at higher rates than any other country," Krug explains in the 1997 CDC publication "Best Practices of Youth Violence Prevention," "No child should die a violent death in the most industrialized country in the world."

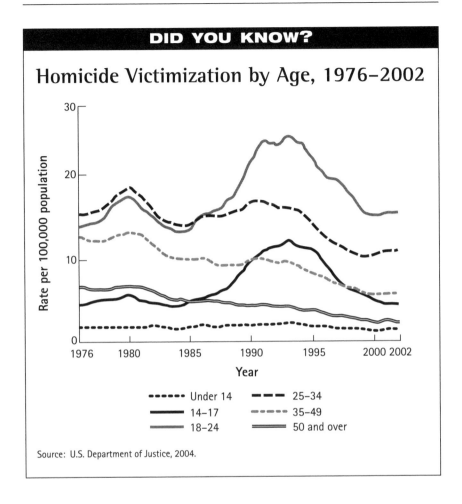

DID YOU KNOW?

Homicide Victimization by Age, 1976–2002

Source: U.S. Department of Justice, 2004.

Young people also account for the majority of perpetrators of violent crime. According to a Uniform Crime Report issued by the Federal Bureau of Investigation (FBI), more than 15,000 murders in 2001 were committed by people aged 13–22; two-thirds of those were young men.

Guns were used to commit seven out of 10 murders in the United States, and death by firearms occurs 12 times more often in the United States than in other industrialized countries. Gun control activist Sarah Brady, whose husband James, press secretary to Ronald Reagan, was shot and permanently disabled in a presidential assassination attempt, notes that handguns kept in the home are 43 times more likely to be used against a family member or friend than against an intruder.

Dr. Krug of the CDC also notes that young people in the United States kill themselves at double the rate of other countries. More than 30,000 people in the United States committed suicide in 2001; 3,971 of these were young people between the ages of 15 and 24, making suicide the third-leading cause of death in this age group. Eighty-six percent of young people who committed suicide in 2001 were male; 14 percent were female. Firearms were used in more than half of all youth suicides.

People over the age of 65 also have very high suicide rates. In 2001, 5,393 people over 65 committed suicide; 85 percent of this group were male. Firearms were used in 73 percent of elderly suicides.

CO-VICTIMS OF HOMICIDE

When a family member dies a violent death, the surviving relatives are often so devastated that grief specialists now refer to them as "co-victims." According to grief specialist Kathleen Gilbert, author of "Traumatic Loss and the Family" in the book *Family Focus on . . . Death and Dying*, traumatic losses deeply overwhelm the resources of the bereaved so that they feel helpless. Grief that results from traumatic loss differs from "normal" grief in a number of ways. Family and friends have no time to anticipate the death. A sense of horror, helplessness, and loss of control affects those who are left behind. Their lives feel disordered, out of joint, and they tend to view the world as a dangerous place. Family members may become obsessed with what the victim went through or the fear he or she may have felt just before death.

Homicide

When a child is murdered, parents often experience profound guilt at having been unable to protect their son or daughter. Because women tend to grieve more openly than men, the mother of the murdered child may feel the father does not really care, leading to marital conflict. Brothers or sisters of the victim may become tremendously fearful for their own safety or for the safety of other siblings. The murder of a husband or wife can be especially devastating, because grieving may be compounded by financial worries or concerns about how to raise children alone. Children who lose a parent to homicide may experience devastating fear and anger, at both the murderer and at the lost parent for not having fought harder or escaped.

In addition to all these overwhelming feelings, families of homicide victims may have to deal with media coverage, police investigations, and trials—all of which can extend the process of grieving. As grief therapist Leslie Gorski explains, co-victims can become very discouraged because criminal and judicial procedures are complex and take a long time to unfold. Victims want answers and justice and they want trials to come about in a timely manner so they can get through it. Unfortunately, for many co-victims, when justice does come, they find it does not heal as they had expected it would and they are left with an even more profound sense of loss.

TEENS SPEAK

My Brother Was Murdered

My older brother Donnie was killed by a rival gang member when I was five. I'm now 19, and just last week Donnie's murderer, Joe Howard, was executed—by lethal injection.

Mom witnessed the execution, but she wouldn't let me go. I've waited so long for this, wishing and hoping for some kind of justice for Donnie. I hardly remember what Donnie looked like anymore, but his murderer's face is as clear as can be in my mind.

The awful thing is, the execution didn't help. I thought I'd feel better, but in some strange way, I feel even worse. Joe's death didn't make the hurt go away, and it didn't bring Donnie back. Now what do I do?

According to Gorski, co-victims "actually don't get better as time goes by—they can actually get worse. They start off very numb. . . That lingers with them for some time. The more unpredictable and unexpected the death is, the longer the individuals left behind stay emotionally anesthetized." Gorski adds that sometimes people outside the family may blame the victim or the family of the victim for what happened, complicating the grieving process.

Brian Canfield, president of the International Association of Marriage and Family Counselors, adds that co-victims may experience grief that is compounded with rage, delaying the healing process substantially. According to a 2002 article, "Group Intervention for Bereavement after Violent Death," in *Psychiatric Services*, 5 percent of family members actually witness the violent death, further complicating grief.

Suicide

Grieving for a family member who has committed suicide may be even more difficult than grieving for a murder victim. While anger against the perpetrator can complicate grieving for co-victims of a homicide, it can also motivate them and give them purpose. When a suicide occurs, however, the perpetrator and the victim are the same, leaving family members feeling even more bereft. Family members may feel guilty that they could not prevent the suicide, and they may feel others are blaming them for what occurred. According to the American Society for Suicide Prevention, however, "90 percent of all people who die by suicide have a diagnosable psychiatric disorder at the time of their death (most often depression or bipolar disorder). Just as people can die of heart disease or cancer, people can die as a consequence of mental illness."

COMPLICATED GRIEF

When grieving does not follow the "normal" pattern, it may be referred to as "pathological" or "complicated" grief. People who lose a loved one to homicide or suicide are much more likely to suffer from this "abnormal" grief than people who are grieving for a loved one who died of natural causes. These people may need professional help to recover.

Professors Holly G. Prigerson and Selby C. Jacobs of the Yale University Department of Psychiatry, authors of "All the Doctors Suddenly Go," a 2001 article in the *Journal of the American Medical Association*, note that this complicated grief is similar to post-traumatic stress disorder (PTSD). As with PTSD, the co-victim of a violent death may obsessively reenact the event, may try to avoid reminders of the victim, and may experience physiological hyperarousal, a very unpleasant, biologically based oversensitivity that can include rapid heart rate, heightened blood sugar, muscle tension, increased sweating, dilated pupils, shallow breathing, choking sensations, shortness of breath, and difficulty concentrating, according to the *American Psychiatric Association Diagnostic and Statistical Manual of Mental Disorders*. Prigerson and Jacobs suggest to family doctors that a patient may be suffering from complicated grief if they regularly exhibit at least three of the following symptoms over a period of more than six months:

■ Intrusive thoughts about the victim

■ Obsessive yearning for the person who has died

■ Searching for the deceased person

■ Excessive loneliness

In addition, the patient must exhibit four of the following symptoms, experienced nearly every day, for more than six months:

■ Numbness or lack of emotion

■ Purposelessness

■ Refusing to believe the death has occurred

■ A feeling that life no longer has meaning

■ A sense that part of oneself has died

■ A feeling of being unable to control or trust

■ Taking on harmful behaviors of the deceased person

■ Excessive anger about the death

Family doctors should refer patients suffering from complicated grief to psychiatric care.

COPING WITH VIOLENT DEATH

In "Traumatic Loss and the Family," Gilbert recommends a number of important tools for families as they attempt to heal from the violent death of someone they love:

■ Open communication, especially making time to listen to one another

■ Shared rituals—religious or personal—to memorialize the victim

■ Shared sense of purpose—this may include the family uniting to work to prevent other violent deaths

■ Acceptance of differences in how family members react to the death

■ Sensitivity to the needs of each family member

■ Trying to focus on the strengths of each family member

Grief therapist Leslie Gorski agrees that communication is crucial to healing. She says that to handle and conquer such a life crisis, "We tell everybody—we tell the police, family, coworkers, friends, neighbors. After a few months, we have told our favorite clerk at the grocery store and the bank teller. Every time we tell the story, we conquer the fear, trauma, and fright . . . That's how we diminish trauma." Not talking about the loss, Gorski emphasizes, can lead to long-term problems. Support groups in which co-victims discuss their loss with other families who have experienced violent death can be particularly helpful.

PREVENTING VIOLENT DEATH

According to the American Foundation for Suicide Prevention, strategies that may help prevent suicide include the following:

- Education. This includes educating professionals on how to recognize people who are at risk for suicide, educating society that people who attempt suicide are usually suffering from a medical condition that can be treated, and educating suicide survivors in the resources available to them.

- Treatment. This includes finding improved ways to identify those at greatest risk for suicide and improving and expanding treatment options as well as making screening for depression part of every physician's routine.

- Gun control. This includes supporting legislation to control access to guns.

Because so many murders are committed with firearms, gun control is also an important aspect of homicide prevention. According to professor Carol Runyon of the University of North Carolina's Injury Prevention Research Center, the following strategies may also help to prevent homicide:

- Therapy. Since many homicides occur as a result of arguments between family members, counseling to help families deal with disagreements could reduce the incidence of homicide.

- Education. This includes violence-prevention curricula in schools, training in conflict resolution in the workplace, and training in parenting skills.

Violent death—homicide and suicide—may be the most devastating form of unexpected loss. For those who are left to mourn, the circumstances often imposes additional physical and emotional complications to the grieving process. Difficult as it may seem, the trauma can be overcome, and therapeutic assistance is available.

See also: Death, Unexpected and Planned; Death and the Family; Death of a Parent; Teenage Deaths; Grieving, the Process of

FURTHER READING
Wolfedt, Alan D. *Healing Your Traumatized Heart: 100 Practical Ideas after Someone You Loved Dies a Violent Death.* Laguna Hills, CA: Companion Press, 2002.

HOTLINES
AND HELP SITES

Aging with Dignity
URL: http://www.agingwithdignity.org
Phone: (888) 594-7437
Mission: To provide information, advice, and legal tools to help people ensure that they receive quality care as they age and that their wishes regarding their care are respected

American Association of Suicidology (AAS)
URL: http://www.suicidology.org
Phone: (202) 237-2280
Mission: To understand and prevent suicide. The AAS promotes research, public awareness programs, public education, and training for professionals and volunteers. In addition, the AAS serves as a national clearinghouse for information on suicide.

American Hospice Foundation
URL: http://www.americanhospice.org
Phone: (202) 233-0204
Mission: To improve access to quality hospice care through public education, professional training and consumer advocacy

Americans for Better Care of the Dying (ABCD)
URL: http://www.abcd-caring.org
Phone: (202) 895-2660
Mission: To ensure that every person experiences comfort, dignity, and meaning at the end of life and that every loved one knows that

life came to a close in a dignified way. By sharing expertise, building collaborative networks and public commitment, the ABCD seeks to achieve substantive health-care reform through improved policy, professional practice, and care reimbursement.

Children's Hospice International
URL: http://www.chionline.org
Phone: (800) 24-CHILD (242-4453)
Mission: To create public awareness of the needs of children with life-threatening conditions and of their families, and of what children's hospice care can do to meet those needs. The organization seeks to include hospice perspectives in all areas of pediatric care and education.

Choice in Dying, Inc.
URL: http://www.choices.org
Phone: (888) 246-4237
Mission: To empower students with vital tools that will increase their career and life opportunities

Compassion in Dying
URL: http://www.compassionindying.org
Phone: (503) 221-9556
Mission: To provide leadership for client services, legal advocacy, and public education to improve pain and symptom management, increase patient empowerment and self-determination and expand end-of-life choices to include aid-in-dying for terminally, mentally competent patients

The Dougy Center for Grieving Children and Their Families
URL: http://www.dougy.org
Phone: (866) 775-5683
Mission: To provide loving support in a safe place so that children, teens, and their families can share their experiences as they move through the healing process

Grief Recovery Online
URL: http://www.groww.org
Mission: To provide support resources for the grieving community. Although the program was originally begun for the widowed, it

became apparent that the need for support for *all* grievers was lacking

Growth House
URL: http://www.growthhouse.org
Phone: (415) 863-3045
Mission: To improve the quality of compassionate care for people who are dying through patient education and global professional collaboration

Mothers Against Drunk Driving (MADD)
URL: http://www.madd.org
Phone: (800) GET-MADD (438-6233)
Mission: To stop drunk driving, support the victims of this violent crime, and prevent underage drinking

Mothers Against Teen Violence
URL: http://www.matvinc.org
Phone: (866) MAT-VINC (628-8462)
Mission: To make schools and communities safer through effective teen violence prevention

National Center for Victims of Crime (NCVC)
URL: http://www.ncvc.org
Phone: (202) 467-8700
Mission: To forge a national commitment to help victims of crime rebuild their lives. The NCVC is dedicated to serving individuals, families, and communities harmed by crime

National Family Caregivers Association (NFCA)
URL: http://www.nfcacares.org
Phone: (800) 896-3650
Mission: To support, empower, educate, and speak up for the more than 50-million Americans who care for a chronically ill, aged, or disabled loved one. The NFCA reaches across the boundaries of different diagnoses, different relationships, and different life stages to address the common needs and concerns of all family caregivers.

National Suicide Hotline
Phone: (800) SUICIDE (784-2433)

Rainbows
URL: http://www.rainbows.org
Phone: (800) 266-3206
Mission: To foster emotional healing among children grieving a loss from a life-altering crisis

Sena Foundation
URL: http://www.sena.org
Phone: (804) 633-7575
Mission: To provide free support for those going through catastrophic loss. In addition to working with those who grieve the death of a loved one, Sena also offers support to those suffering loss issues resulting from aging, divorce, rape, substance abuse, and other social problems not commonly associated with grief and loss

Tragedy Assistance Program for Survivors (T*A*P*S)
URL: http://www.taps.org
Phone: (800) 959-TAPS (8277)
Mission: To assist families of members of the military who have suffered a loss by bringing together survivors who can share grief and derive strength from one another

Well Spouse Foundation
URL: http://www.wellspouse.org
Phone: (800) 838-0873
Mission: To give support to wives, husbands, and partners of the chronically ill or disabled

GLOSSARY

accident   an event that causes injury or death and by definition, cannot be anticipated or avoided; also called unintentional injury

advance directive   a legal document that indicates how a person wants health-care decisions made at the end of his or her life

ageism   discrimination against a person because of his or her age

algor mortis   a steady decline in the temperature of a body following death

anorexia nervosa   an eating disorder that leads to self-imposed starvation

apnea   a temporary absence or cessation of breathing

autoimmune disease   a disease in which the body seems to attack itself. AIDS, lupus, Crohn's disease, and rheumatoid arthritis are autoimmune diseases

autopsy   literally "to see for oneself"; a postmortem examination of a body to determine the cause of death

bioethicist   a person who studies the ethical and moral implications of biological research

brain death   a state in which there is a cessation of brain function but the body is kept alive by artificial means

cancer   a disease in which cells in the body grow abnormally and uncontrollably

cardiopulmonary resuscitation (CPR)   a series of interventions to restart a stopped heart (including electric shock and drugs)

casket   a rectangular box used to bury a body; the connotation is something more elaborate than a coffin

centenarians   people who are at least 100 years old

cerebrovascular diseases   strokes and other diseases that affect the blood flow to the brain

chemotherapy   the chemical treatment of disease, especially cancer

coffin   a plain box or chest for burying a body

columbaria   underground vaults with niches designed to hold urns containing human ashes

coma   a state of deep, prolonged unconsciousness, caused by injury or disease

congenital malformations   deformations and chromosomal abnormalities that occur as a fetus develops

crematory   a place where dead bodies are burned

dementia   progressive mental deterioration, including memory loss, confusion, reduction of the ability to handle everyday tasks, and variations in alertness

desensitization   a loss in sensitivity occasioned by repeated exposure to stimuli; used to describe becoming accustomed to violence through seeing images of violence in the media

diabetes a chronic disease characterized by the body's failure to properly use or make the hormone insulin, resulting in too much sugar in the blood

do-not-resuscitate order (DNR) an order from a physician on a terminally ill patient's chart instructing health-care providers not to attempt to restore the person in the event of heart or respiratory failure

electroencephalograms (EEG) a device used to record electrical activity in the brain

embalming the prevention of body decomposition through the use of chemical processes

euthanasia the putting to death by a painless method of a terminally ill person; from the Greek for "easy death"

geriatrics the medical specialty of caring for the elderly

gerontologist one who studies the process and problems of aging

homicide the killing of one human being by another

hospice a way of providing care to terminally ill patients that focuses on managing pain and allowing the patient to die a peaceful death, often at home

inhumation method of disposing of dead bodies by burial in the earth

intestate dying without a will

legacy money or property left to someone by a will

living will a detailed statement that indicates the medical treatment a person wants if he or she is terminally ill and unable to make decisions for himself or herself

malignant neoplasms cancerous growths

mortality the nature of humankind, as eventually having to die

Medicare a federal health-insurance program for people 65 and older and certain disabled people under 65

mortician funeral director

mourning the public behaviors that accompany grief; the period of time during which grieving occurs

nephritis/nephrosis inflammation of the kidneys

organ transplantation in a surgical operation, moving an organ from one organism to another

palliative care treatment to relieve pain rather than a disease

pathological due to or related to a disease

physician–assisted suicide (PAS) a situation in which a physician assists a person who wants to die by writing a prescription for a lethal dose of drugs; legal in the United States only in Oregon

postmortem after death

psychosomatic illness an illness brought on by the influence of the mind

pyre a heaped pile of wood on which a body is burned

respite care temporary care provided by a nursing home, assisted-living facility, or other institution which allows family caregivers to take time off from caring for ill relatives

right-to-life movement of people who oppose abortion

rigor mortis the stiffening of a body after death

sarcophagus a stone coffin

senile pertaining to old age

septicemia a disease caused by microorganisms or toxins in the blood; also called blood poisoning

subsyndromal depression a form of depression that affects up to one in four seniors, characterized by depressive symptoms that affect well-being and quality of life but do not meet the criteria for major depression

suicide the taking of one's own life

suttee the burning of a widow on her husband's funeral pyre; now outlawed in India

terminal illness the final stages of a fatal disease

Totten Trust a "pay on death" trust account in which a person places money to be used after death, as for funerals

ventilator a machine used to maintain breathing; also known as a respirator

will a legal document declaring a person's wishes regarding the disposal of his or her property after death

INDEX

Page numbers in **boldface** indicate extensive coverage of a topic. Page numbers in *italic* indicate graphs or sidebars.